The Wood Chair in America

SO-BMW-110

Produced, Designed and Edited by
Donovan and Green

Written with
C. Ray Smith and Marian Page

Published by
Estelle D. Brickel and
Stephen B. Brickel, New York

65707

Woodbury University Library
1027 Wilshire Boulevard
Los Angeles, California 90017

DISCARDED

Library of Congress Cataloging in Publication Data
The Wood Chair in America
1. Chairs — United States — History
2. Page, Marian, 1918-
I. Smith, C. Ray
II. Donovan and Green
TS886.5.C45W66   1982   684.1'3
Library of Congress Catalog Card Number 82-90454
ISBN 0-9609844-0-2

**Copyright © 1982 by Estelle D. Brickel and
Stephen B. Brickel**
All rights reserved. No part of this publication may be re
duced in any form or by any means, without the prior wr
permission of the publisher.

Published by Estelle D. Brickel and Stephen B. Bricke
Printed in the United States of America

Produced and Designed by:
Michael Donovan and Nancye Green, Donovan and Gree

Edited by:
Nancye Green

Design and Production Coordinator:
Jane Zash, Donovan and Green

Editorial Assistance:
Lauretta Harris, Donovan and Green

Illustrations:
Norman Diekman, Randall Lieu, Jim Silks

Photography:
Amos T.S. Chan, Michael Pateman

Manuscript Consultants:
Marvin Schwartz, William W. Stahl, Jr.

This book is dedicated
to the memory of

Jack Brickel

Founder of
Brickel Associates Inc.

Acknowledgments

The publisher wishes to thank the following people for their participation in the creation of this book:

Ward Bennett
Joseph Bernstein
Amos T.S. Chan
Norman Diekman
Michael Donovan
Horace Enger
Rochelle Feuer
Nancye Green
Lauretta Harris
Randall Lieu
Carl Meyer
Marian Page
Michael Pateman
Marvin Schwartz
Jim Silks
C. Ray Smith
Robert Smith
William W. Stahl, Jr.
Jane Zash

Publisher's Foreword

The Wood Chair in America has been prepared with consideration and love for the craft of chair design and manufacturing.

My first introduction to well-designed chairs came at an early age when my father, Jack Brickel, worked for Herman Miller Inc. I was exposed to the designs of Charles Eames and Alexander Girard; I also became aware of the work of Eero Saarinen, and the designs being introduced by Knoll International and many other fine companies.

For the past 18 years I have had the pleasure of bringing my love for the craft of furniture making, to the manufacturing of Ward Bennett's designs through our company, Brickel Associates Inc. This book, which has been more than two years in the making, represents our commitment to informing and broadening the knowledge of those people who are interested in our craft. At the same time, it offers an argument for our belief that good design is a distillation of the past.

As we are faced today with greater challenges in producing quality handmade products, we are more committed than ever to the tradition of excellence which is our heritage.

Stephen B. Brickel

Preface

Of all the furniture that Western civilization has constructed and coveted throughout its history, the chair is the single item that has been admired and desired in all eras. More than tables, cupboards, and chests of drawers, more than any other furniture in the house, except perhaps the bed itself, the chair has held the place of honor.

From the simplest beginnings to the most elaborate mannerists of our day, no matter what ledge, bench, or banquette might be chiseled into an integral wall, a chair as a freestanding movable object — or that backless chair, the stool — has remained indispensable. From the throne of ceremony to the throne of privacy, the chair is the one item for which there is no substitute and every necessity. It has captured the imaginations of centuries and of civilizations, and has engaged the hands of millions of craftsmen.

The history of chairs therefore contains a microcosm of the history of ideas. The chair has been as much a part of the popular imagination as any other artifact of civilization. It has changed as often as clothing, since it has as much to do with the human body as clothes do.

Through the different stylistic periods, the thrones of Everyman have been alternately simple and ornate, hefty and trim, carved and ornamented with great invention and variety, or distilled to the purest functional essentials. Woods of every kind have been employed, both for structural elements and for decorative overlays or inlays. Wood has the longest and richest tradition in the design and making of chairs throughout history. Wood stands for the memory of life, for vitality itself; its longevity is represented by ring grains and its variety by color and texture.

For decades, American chairs were looked on by foreigners as merely crude copies of English or French models. But increasingly in the past century, furniture experts the world over have come to recognize and to define the distinct national flavor brought to chair design by American makers and craftsmen — whatever that flavor may be.

To chronicle the wood chair in America, this book is divided into four periods, corresponding roughly to the history of America by centuries: Early American, Federal, Victorian, and Modern.

What results is a history of the wood chair in America with an unusually broad and inclusive depiction of styles over more than three centuries. Forty styles and illustrated examples have been chosen, although numerous interesting chairs and chair makers are necessarily excluded from a distillation such as this. Most authorities concentrate on only one or two periods of this history. This book aims to give an inclusive — if by no means so detailed — chronicle of the development of American chairs in wood.

Each period is preceded by an introduction that outlines the themes and general directions of its era. Following that are the successive styles, each represented by a single chair that has been selected as a notable example. Variations within these styles sometimes accompany the major illustrations. The text describes the principal chair design illustrated as an example of its particular style, catalogues the woods of which it was made, and outlines the chairmakers involved in the design and production of its type.

Following this historical section is an illustrated glossary of terms used throughout the book, concluding with a photo essay on a contemporary manufacturing process. Accompanied by a design statement by designer Ward Bennett, this section illustrates a method that utilizes both traditional and modern processes to produce today's handcrafted chairs.

The parade of wood chairs in American history is impressive and revealing, and the promise of its tradition in the future is great.

Table of Contents

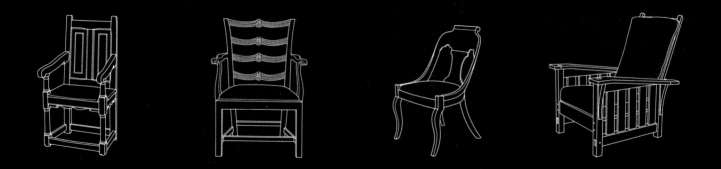

American chairs provide an illuminating document in the history of a people. From the very first days of settlement in the 17th century, American craftsmen produced distinctive designs that reflected the English influence. Subsequent changes suggest how the colonies developed into a nation.

The first chairs were of timeless designs that were close to English provincial forms, but in the course of the Colonial era fashionable trends affected American makers. While consistently aware of Old World models, the American colonists favored forms that were bolder and often simpler than those that provided their inspiration. Local woods were used more for early chairs than those made at the Eve of the Revolution when mahogany was popular. But regardless of the choice of wood, it was a distinctive American aesthetic that determined chair designs.

In the first decades of settlement, turned spindle back (popularly called Carver and Brewster), ladder back or slat back, and wainscot chairs were characteristic—evidence of the persistent popularity of medieval and late Renaissance models in provincial as well as colonial centers.

By the 1690s, the gap between London and Colonial design was narrowing. The richer, more elaborate designs in the William and Mary style were introduced only a decade or so after they were first known in England (1690-1730). Carved backs and front legs were fashionable embellishments on chairs that were thinner in proportion.

During the Queen Anne period (1730-1760), which also arrived a few decades later in the colonies, there was a radical change with chairs smaller in scale. Curving animal form legs, called cabriole legs, replaced the earlier columnar designs, and seats were more often horseshoe-shaped than rectangular, an expression of the flamboyant but human-scaled Rococo style characteristic of the 18th century.

A second phase of the Rococo, the Chippendale style, was more elaborate. The basic curving design was more apt to have carved ornament. The simpler yoke-shaped back of the Queen Anne gave way to one with upturned ends (ears) and the solid splat was replaced by the pierced splat. A significant source was a book of furniture designs by the man for whom the style was named, Thomas Chippendale's *The Gentleman and Cabinet-Maker's Director.* American craftsmen produced elegantly carved chairs in a broad variety of patterns, some directly from the Chippendale book, some from other collections of designs, and some that must have been pure inventions, on the whole simpler and more straightforward than English models.

In the 1760s regional differences in designs of American chairs become most apparent. Philadelphia examples were the most elaborate, Boston the most delicate and New York the heaviest. Examples made in the larger centers were often closer to London fashion than those made in small towns in New England or the South.

The Windsor is a type of simple painted chair that was introduced in the colonies before 1740 and remained popular for close to a century. Its name is from the town in Berkshire, England, where it originated, but it became typically American, used inside and out as a utilitarian form and made of a variety of local woods. Produced first in colonial shops in cities like Philadelphia and New York, the Windsor bridged the eras before and after the Revolution, and in the early 19th century it was the product of the first chair factories.

The colonial era was one of great development as the American colonies emerged as a nation. In chairs this development is paralleled. The first American chairs were simple, very provincial designs that bore little resemblance to fashionable English models. The later American Chippendale examples were elegantly made but distinctive chairs, different from, but the counterpart of, London efforts.

Wainscot Panel Back
1640-1700

In 17th-century America as in medieval Europe, chairs were rare. When they did exist they were considered seats of honor, frequently listed in household inventories as "Great Chayres." The boldly carved detail (right), of rosettes under a flat cresting rail of segments of arches, is from the top of wainscot chair now at the Museum of Fine Arts, Boston.

A typical wainscot chair is the Pierson Chair (right) with its framed back enclosing two vertical fielded panels. The scroll shape on the underside of the sloping arms is reiterated under the seat frame. This chair was taken to the Collegiate School at Saybrook, Connecticut, by the Reverend Abraham Pierson when he became Rector in 1701. Ever since it has been the presidential chair of that school, known today as Yale University, where it resides.

Materials: The Pierson chair, like most wainscots, is made of oak. The name derives from the Dutch *wagonschot*, meaning a fine oak plank.

Makers: Joiners, rather than turners, usually made wainscot chairs because of their skill in framed panel construction. Most joiners of the period were anonymous, but a carved wainscot chair belonging to Bowdoin College has been attributed to William Searle, a joiner at Ipswich, Massachusetts.

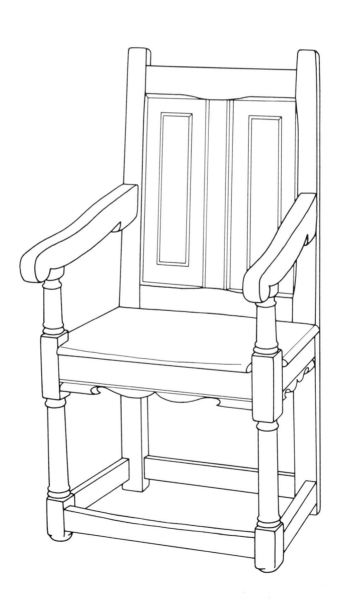

Carver Spindle Back
1650-1670

Early post-and-spindle chairs, such as the Carver and Brewster chairs, were made by turners who used gouges and chisels to shape wood while it rotated on pedal-operated lathes.

Carver chairs take their name from the first governor of Plymouth, Massachussets, who is believed to have owned the one now in Pilgrim Hall. The Carver-type chair, with ball-turned rear stiles and arm supports, vase-and-ball turned spindles, acorn-shaped finials, and ball-shaped handholds, relates to the Lowlands tradition of elaborate turnery. Grooves marking the alignment of rungs, spindles, arms, seat rails, and stretchers are used as decoration. Whereas Carver chairs usually have turned spindles only on the back, the similar Brewster chair also has turned spindles that go below the seat rail.

Materials: This rush-seated Carver chair is of maple; ash, elm, and hickory were also used for such chairs. The seats were sometimes of plain wood or splints.

Makers: The chair illustrated is in the Garvan Collection at Yale; it may have originated in either the Dutch Settlements of the Hudson River Valley or in a New England shop.

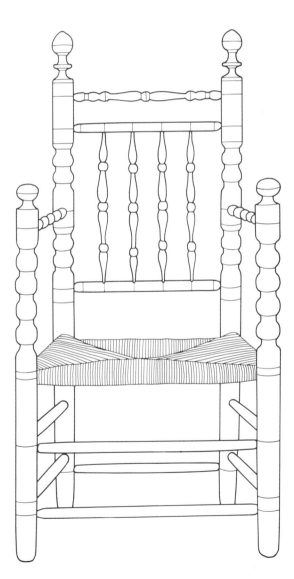

Cromwellian Leather
1650-1680

The joint stool (right) was the precursor of the armless Cromwellian chair. Its name is derived from the jointed, mortise-and-tenon method of construction. These stools may also have been used as occasional tables.

A Cromwellian side chair, which may have been fitted with a padded leather cushion, is identifiable by its stretchers, spindles, and uprights, which are rope turned. More common is a leather-upholstered back panel. The Colonial Cromwell chair was patterned after a small chair with leather-covered seat and back panel, popular in England during Cromwell's time. This had replaced the joint stool that, it is thought, was used at dining tables. Colonial Cromwell chairs were similarly used by the fashionable and well-to-do.

Materials: Cromwellian chairs were often maple, although this chair is of walnut and white oak. Seats and backs were covered in leather or needlework, which was attached with studs nailed into the chair frame.

Makers: Makers of Cromwellian chairs are not known. This side chair came from Crosswick's Creek, now White Horse, New Jersey, and is in the collection of the Philadelphia Museum of Art.

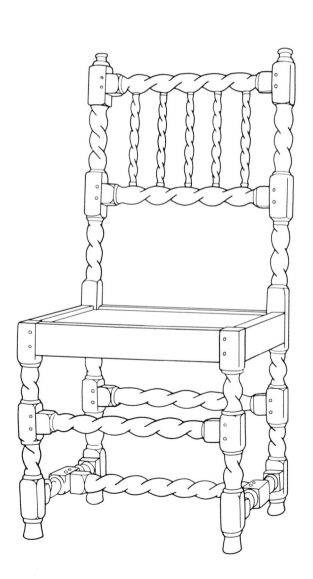

**William and Mary
Banister Back
1690-1730**

Banister back chairs, typical of the William and Mary style popular in 18th-century America, showed great variety in their ornamentally carved crests and the sometimes intricate turning of their banisters.

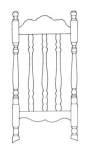

A banister back chair is a simplified version of the tall-back William and Mary style, which was introduced to England after 1689. The illustrated armchair has a series of split banisters, also called balusters, in its back, topped by pierced and carved cresting; it has ram's-horn arms, block-and-vase turned legs, four bulbous stretchers, and Spanish feet. Within the variety of banisters made during this period, some are flat or true split banisters — that is, one half of a round banister; the flat side was usually placed facing front for comfort.

Materials: With a seat made of rush instead of cane, the frame of this banister back is dark-painted maple — the principal wood used in banister backs.

Makers: The makers of such chairs are unknown, and even the geographic location of their manufacture is often conjecture. This chair is in the Hammond-Harwood House in Annapolis, Maryland, and dates from about 1700 to 1725.

William and Mary
1690-1730

Pioneer days were a fading memory for the craftsmen who fashioned the tall-back, vertically proportioned cane chairs that began to grace Colonial parlors in the 1690s. Pierced crests, introduced during this period, are common details of William and Mary chairs.

High backs and caning are typical of the William and Mary style. Flattened cresting and rounded arms indicate the New England origin of this example, a transitional piece that displays an early use of the carbriole leg and stretchers shaped like the turnings found on Connecticut side chairs of the later Queen Anne period.

Materials: This chair is of painted maple and cane. Walnut was also used for William and Mary caned chairs, which were often painted black.

Makers: Makers of chairs in the William and Mary style are rarely known. Chairmaker John Gaines of Portsmouth, New Hampshire, however, is known for chairs that show a Queen Anne influence but have many points of the William and Mary style. This chair was probably made in New England between 1700 and 1725.

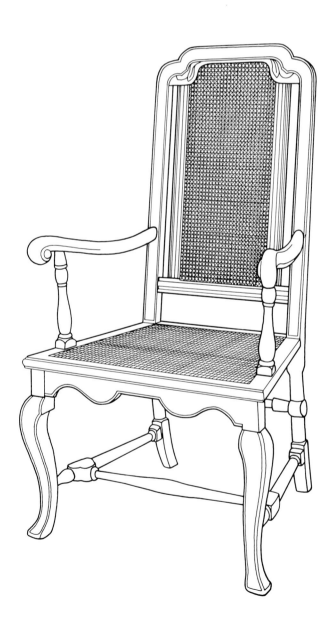

New England Slat Back
1700-1800

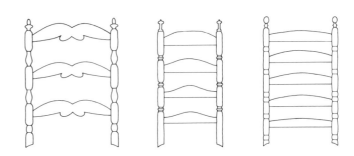

The 18th-century slat back was a modification of earlier and heavier 17th-century slat backs, which usually had only two or three slats. The 18th-century version rarely had fewer than four, was lighter, and had a higher back.

A typical 18th-century slat back armchair made in New England has five graduated, gently-arched slats, lemon-shaped finials, serpentine arms, and a rush seat. Front stretchers are sausage turned; the side and rear ones plain. Stiles and front legs have ring-shaped turnings. Slat backs (sometimes called ladder backs) had a long tradition. Later they were given an elegant transformation by Chippendale and Sheraton; the Shakers gave the tradition a new vigor in the 19th century.

Materials: This chair is of maple with hickory slats, seat rails, and stretchers. Most slat-back chairs had rush seats and were originally painted. Traces of both black and green paint remain on this one.

Makers: The slat back was a favorite of both city and country chairmakers throughout the 18th century, but individual makers are generally unknown. This New England example is in the Garvan Collection at Yale.

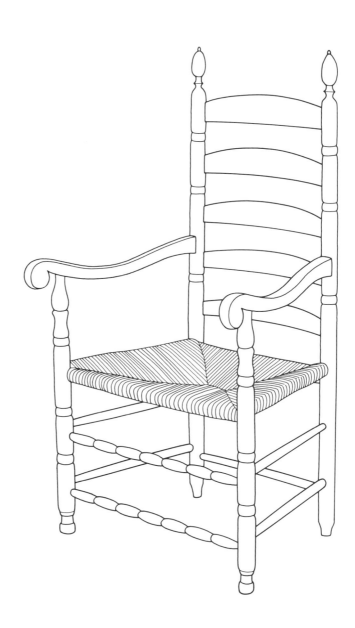

Queen Anne Fiddle Back
1730-1760

Carved shells on crest rails or on knees of cabriole legs, an important detail of the Queen Anne style, were crafted with considerable variety and invention. Those illustrated left to right are from the crest rails of: a side chair attributed to John Goddard of Newport, a Philadelphia side chair, and an armchair by William Savery of Philadelphia.

The cabriole legs and the curved shaping of stiles, rails, seat, spoon-shaped supports, and vase-shaped splat (called fiddle back in the Colonies) mark a typical Queen Anne armchair. The style reached America several years after the death of the English queen in 1714, when curves began to dominate the design of chairs for the first time. The extravagance of the front curves of this chair in contrast to the severely plain stump rear legs indicates a Philadelphia origin. Leaf forms at the front of the knees and scrolls at the ends of the arms are the only relief ornament.

Materials: This chair is of mahogany. Walnut, maple, and cherry were also used.

Makers: Chairmakers were only beginning to be known by name. The best known in the Queen Anne style is probably William Savery of Philadelphia. John Gaines of Portsmouth, New Hampshire, worked during the period, but no chairs that he made purely in this style have been identified.

**Queen Anne Corner
1725-1760**

Corner chairs, used for writing and, it is thought, at the card table, may have been designed to accommodate the hooped, pannier skirts that became fashionable in the 18th century.

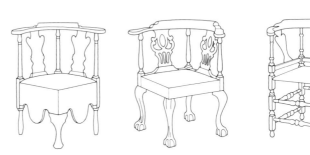

Straight block-and-vase-turned legs and the absence of splats mark this New England corner chair as a country example of its type, which achieved popularity in the Colonies during the Queen Anne period. Sausage-turned stretchers join the legs, which terminate in pad-and-disc feet. Later versions of Queen Anne corner chairs (sometimes called roundabout chairs) have vase-shaped or pierced splats, often deep aprons (to conceal chamber pots), and cabriole legs with claw-and-ball feet (above). Corner chairs were made in England and on the Continent, as well as in America, during the 18th century.

Materials: Maple was used for this example. Other corner chairs were of walnut and mahogany.

Makers: Dated between 1725 and 1740, this New England corner chair is in the collection of the Winterthur Museum. Makers have not been identified.

Connecticut Chippendale
1750-1790

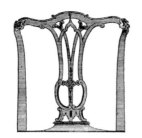

Great variations in pierced splats were produced in American Chippendale chairs, which were derived, however carefully or crudely realized, from the illustrations (right) in Thomas Chippendale's The Gentleman and Cabinet-Maker's Director.

The simple carved shell on its crest rail, the plain uncarved knees, and the continuation of the crest rail into the splat differentiate the simple Connecticut armchair from a more elaborate Philadelphia counterpart, which it resembles in overall design. The serpentine arms with scrolled handholds, the crest rail with scrolled ears, and the stump rear legs follow the general outline of Philadelphia chairs and are evidence of its maker's apprenticeship in that city. Cabriole legs with claw-and-ball feet (as seen here) and Marlborough legs were both characteristic of Chippendale chairs.

Materials: Cherry was used for this Connecticut-made chair instead of the mahogany or black walnut used in Philadelphia Chippendales.

Makers: Attributed to Eliphalet Chapin circa 1780, this chair is in the Garvan Collection at Yale. Chapin apprenticed in Philadelphia before returning in 1771 to his native Connecticut to open a shop in East Windsor.

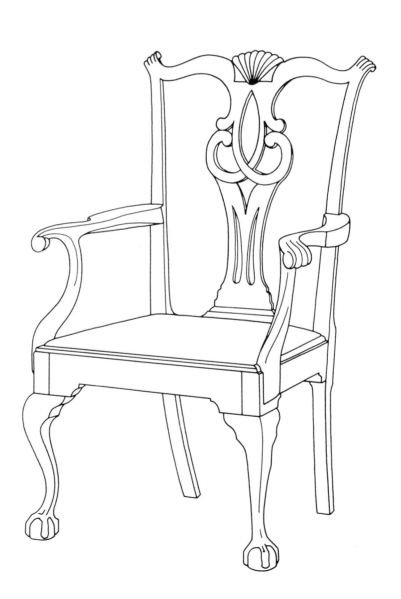

Windsor Sack Back
1740-1820

One of the most popular types is the writing-arm (right), which prefigures the functional school chair of the nineteenth and twentieth centuries. Jefferson is supposed to have written the Declaration of Independence on such a chair.

Sack back Windsor chairs (sometimes called bow backs) have their arm rails topped by a bow-shaped piece of wood. New England Windsors such as this have no foot; the lower part of the leg is shaped like a long cone, with ring and vase-shaped turnings above it. Instead of stiles from floor to crest rail, as in almost all previous chairs, a Windsor has a plank seat, which serves as a leg-supported platform from which the other elements rise. Although Windsors seem to have originated in 15th-century Gothic England, they achieved their greatest beauty in America.

Materials: Windsor chairs were made of a variety of woods and were almost always painted. In this chair, top rail, arm rail, and spindles are of white oak; the seat is pine; legs, stretchers, and arm supports are birch.

Makers: Windsors were made both by specialists and by craftsmen all along the Atlantic coast between 1740-1820. This chair, in the Garvan Collection at Yale, was probably made in New England circa 1765-1795.

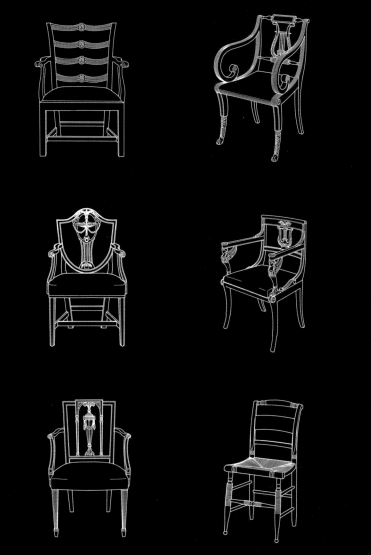

Federal—Neoclassical
1785-1830

After the Revolution, it is interesting to see that independence brought with it a greater dependence upon English design. The time gap was reduced as communications improved and the number of style-conscious, affluent Americans increased. The period known as Federal, predominantly neoclassical in style, developed as a reaction to the Rococo. While the Rococo was a play on traditional classical motifs, the Neoclassical was based on the idea of reviving the use of ancient classical motifs. It was a style inspired by archaeological discoveries made in the 18th century, having great meaning to Americans who were investigating ancient Greek Republican concepts and ancient Roman theories of democracy.

Revolutionary designers had preceded the revolutionary theorists in France and England, but by the time Americans were ready for the new styles, there were popular sources in design books like George Hepplewhite's *Guide*

of 1788 and Thomas Sheraton's *Drawing Book* of 1791-4.

Federal chairs were made in a variety of designs with ornament generally delicate but rich. Straight lines and simple curves were embellished with fine inlays or carving in low relief on rectangular-backed and shield back chairs. The influence of ancient design was made more apparent by some designers who adapted the Greek klismos form, used so beautifully by the most famous American cabinetmaker of the Federal period, Duncan Phyfe.

American craftsmen achieved elegance by using fine woods, particularly mahogany. Following contemporary fashion, they made very stylish and elaborate painted pieces. Stylish design was also important to chairmakers producing simpler work. Windsor chairmakers made what was called Fancy Painted Sheraton chairs in which pine, maple and hickory were used to produce

designs based on the ancient klismos form. These painted chairs were the first to be mass-produced in factories like the one established by Lambert Hitchcock of Hitchcocksville, Connecticut.

While designers concentrated on neoclassicism in the Federal era there was a change of taste as delicate early forms were replaced by heavier and larger scaled designs, in proportion to the high ceilinged Greek Revival rooms. Some of this change is attributed to the influence of the French Empire designs introduced by architects and artists employed by Napoleon. By 1830, it was large-scaled klismos chairs, with relatively heavy lionspaw feet, or executed quite simply without carved decoration, that were characteristic. New York was one of the centers of elegant furniture production, but fine work was made in every major center, and places like Boston, Philadelphia, Salem and Baltimore had shops producing distinctive designs.

Federal Ladder Back
1785-1800

The plain slat back chair became the graceful ladder back at the hands of Chippendale and was later interpreted by Sheraton. The more usual Chippendale ladders sometimes have interlaced and intertwined designs like Chippendale splats (right).

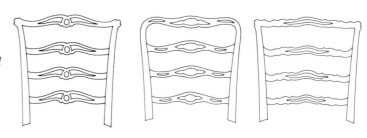

A sophisticated adaptation of the earlier slat back chair, the ladder back appeared toward the end of the 18th century while the Chippendale style waned in popularity. This transitional ladder back armchair has an overall Chippendale style — with straight Marlborough legs — but the ladders are draped, and the openwork slats are centered by a medallion that is cut out to form a spray of feathers. This detail suggests a Sheraton Neoclassical influence.

Materials: Mahogany with an upholstered slip seat. Mahogany was the primary wood used in most cabinet-making centers during the Federal period.

Makers: This particular ladder of draped and openwork slats is sometimes attributed to Daniel Trotter of Philadelphia, who worked in both Chippendale and classic revival styles.

Hepplewhite Shield Back
1790-1810

Swags, urns, drapery, sheaves of wheat, and Prince of Wales feathers are among the carved decorations that vary the shield backs of American Hepplewhite chairs. They took their inspiration from the drawings in Hepplewhite's The Cabinet-Maker and Upholsterer's Guide *(right).*

This American adaptation of a design in George Hepplewhite's *Guide* has a shield-shaped back with a serpentine crest rail, which is carved. The carved-and-pierced splat has a cylix cup framed in an oval with festoons of leaves. At the base of the splat is a carved basket of fruit. The tapering legs are fluted. Hepplewhite emphasized fine inlay, square tapering legs, and backs that were shaped as shields, hearts, or ovals.

Materials: Mahogany was used for this chair as it was for most chairs during this period.

Makers: Owned by the Boston Museum of Fine Arts, this armchair is attributed to Samuel McIntire, architect-carver of Salem, Massachusetts, who was one of the important chairmakers of the Federal period and probably the first American architect to design furniture for his houses. The carved basket of fruit is a recognized McIntire trademark, although it was used by others.

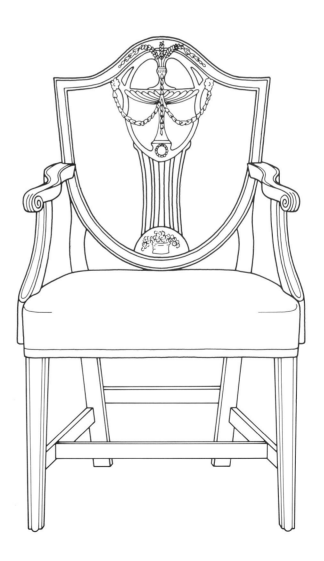

Sheraton Square Back
1800-1820

Variants of the Sheraton square back as illustrated in Thomas Sheraton's Drawing Book *(right), were made in Salem, Boston, Philadelphia, and Baltimore, each of which tended to favor different models. The left variation was favored by New Yorkers and the right by Philadelphians.*

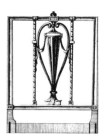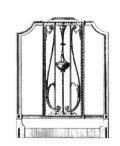

Based on plate 36, no. 1, in the 1794 edition of Thomas Sheraton's *Drawing Book*, this Federal square-back armchair has a center splat carved with drapery and Prince of Wales feathers. Sometimes the carving was interpreted in inlay. Front legs, tapered and reeded, terminate in spade feet. Sheraton preferred square backs and recommended turned and reeded legs. However, Sheraton and Hepplewhite characteristics were often intermingled by American as well as English craftsmen.

Materials: Mahogany was used for this chair, as it was the principal wood used during this period, often contrasted with decorative inlays.

Makers: Made in New York around 1800, the urn-and-drapery back is typical of New York Sheraton square backs, as is the fastening of the arms or elbows into the side seat rails. The chair is in the collection of the Henry Ford Museum. Attributions are extremely difficult since one chairmaker sometimes made frames for another.

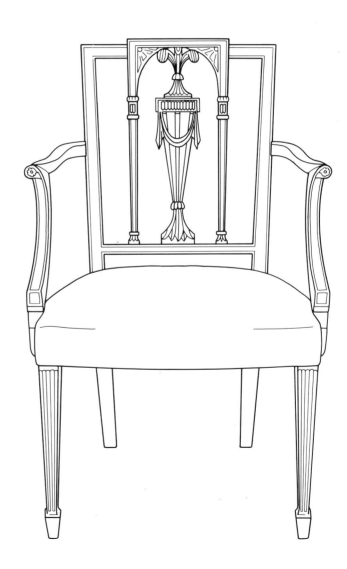

Duncan Phyfe Lyre Back
1800-1820

A strong influence on Phyfe's work was the Greek klismos chair, symbolic of the ancient style, introduced by the French during the Directoire. It had incurved saber legs and a concavely curved back. The sketch (right) includes a chair with saber legs, clearly derived from the klismos form.

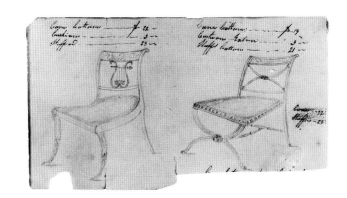

Concave saber-shaped curves appear in every line and outline of this armchair except the seat. The lyre motif, with its scrollwork, rests on a reeded rung. Reeding on arms, side rails, and seat rails is typically Sheraton; lyre splat, hairy legs, and dog-paw feet — similar to lion's-paw feet — are typically Empire. Other typical Phyfe designs include side chairs of curule design, and saber-legged lyre-back side chairs, as in the sketch (above) attributed to Phyfe.

Materials: Mahogany with upholstered seat.

Makers: Scottish-born Duncan Phyfe operated a shop in New York City from 1795 to 1847. This design, made around 1815 and attributed to him, is in the collection of the Henry Ford Museum. Phyfe's long and productive career reached from the delicate Hepplewhite-Adamesque styles to the Empire styles, which he made no pretense of liking. He produced Empire because of the demand but described it as "butcher furniture."[1]

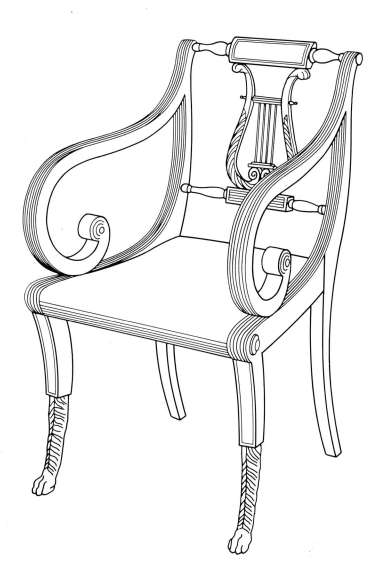

Empire—
Charles Honoré Lannuier
1803-1819

The French cabinetmaker Charles Honoré Lannuier used two types of labels for his furniture, a simple printed paper sticker and an engraved one. Both were in English and French framed by two pillars with a pedimented top.

Winged and gilded caryatid arm supports, gilt ornament centered on the crest rail, a lyre splat with gilded water-leaf motif at its base—all in true French Empire style—betray the maker's Paris origin. Lannuier used these classical details to evoke the archaeological digs into ancient Greece and Rome, which had been explored under the French Empire. Water-leaf carving on front legs is not visible. The French lyre splat is both wider and more open than Phyfe's elongated lyre. While Lannuier brought the French style directly to his New York-made chairs, he also followed English styles.

Materials: Mahogany with black, gilt, and ormolu decoration.

Makers: French-born Charles Honoré Lannuier arrived in New York in 1803 and produced chairs more elaborate than those of Phyfe. This is one of a set ordered from Lannuier around 1815 by Baltimore merchant James Bosley. It is in the collection of the Maryland Historical Society.

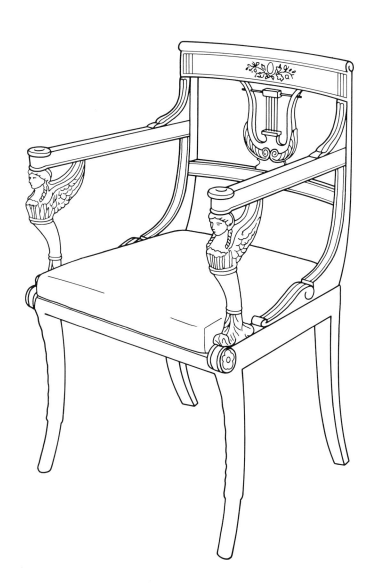

Lambert Hitchcock — Fancy
1825-1843

Variations in the stenciled backs of Hitchcock "fancy" chairs include the bolster-topped (a), pillow topped (b), crown top (c), and button back (d).

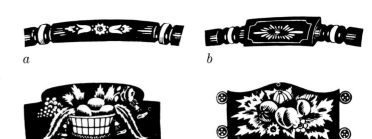

a   b

c   d

This typical Hitchcock "fancy" chair has a slat back, a bolster top, and tapering ring-turned front legs. The stenciled design of fruit and leaves on the turned top rail and wide splat is not shown. The slightly bent back posts are decorated with painted arrows. Hitchcock started making chair parts in 1818 using water-powered machinery. Success led him to the mass production of fully assembled "fancy chairs" with stenciled designs. In 1825 he built a factory at Hitchcocksville, Conn.; by 1826, 100 workers were making chairs. Children painted the first coat (always red) and then women decorated them.

Materials: Maple and hickory painted black with stenciled design in burnished tones of bronze. The rush seat is painted gray. Later Hitchcock fancy chairs had cane or solid plank seats.

Makers: This chair, circa 1825, is in the collection of the Henry Ford Museum. It is marked "L. Hitchcock, Hitchcocksville, Conn. Warranted."

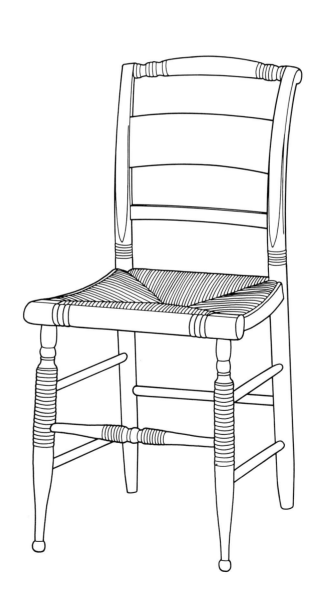

Boston Rocker
1825-1865

The earliest Boston Rockers had simple rosettes painted at the curved ends of their crest rails (illustration below). Later rockers had a curled leaf added to the rosette (top left). The leaf became more elaborate until about 1835 when it was painted without the rosette (top right).

The popular Boston rocker appeared in New England in the second quarter of the 19th century, but how it got its name is a mystery. Some believe that Lambert Hitchcock made the first one in his Connecticut factory. In any case the style soon appeared in all regions of the country and was invariably called a Boston rocker. Its derivation seems to be the tall-back New England Windsor. It has a heavily rolled seat shaped like a cyma curve (the front rolls down, the back rolls up), arms that follow the curve of the seat, seven to nine spindles in its high back, and is usually painted and stenciled.

Materials: Boston rockers are almost always made of maple with pine seats, as is the one shown here, which is painted, grained, and stenciled; its arms were left unpainted.

Makers: Boston rockers were made by the Hitchcock factory in Connecticut and by many unidentified chairmakers in all parts of the country. The illustrated chair from New England, dating from about 1832, is in the collection of the Henry Ford Museum.

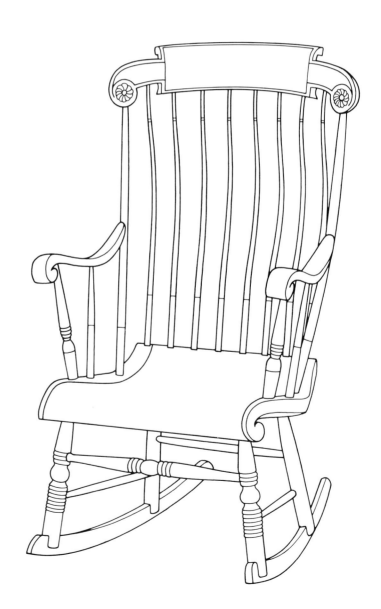

**Late Empire — Zanzibar
1830-1840**

The late Empire style is popularly known as pillar-and-scroll, a name that derives from the extensive use of columns as supports for tables, and of scrolls for chair arms and support elements of other furniture.

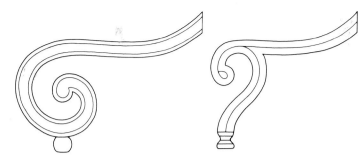

This armchair with turned and reeded legs, and with a caned back and seat, belongs to the concluding phase of Neoclassicism in America. It is known in New England seaport towns as the Zanzibar chair, because, it has been said, of its English prototype and association with the island of Zanzibar, a British protectorate on the Eastern coast of Africa that was important in the clipper ship trade of the early 1800s. Scrolled arms are a fundamental detail of late Empire chairs and sofas.

Materials: Ebonized mahogany and cane with seat pillow.

Makers: This chair was appropriately made in the clipper ship ports of Salem or Boston around 1830. Late Empire chairs were also produced by Joseph Meeks and Sons, and by Duncan Phyfe in New York City, among others.

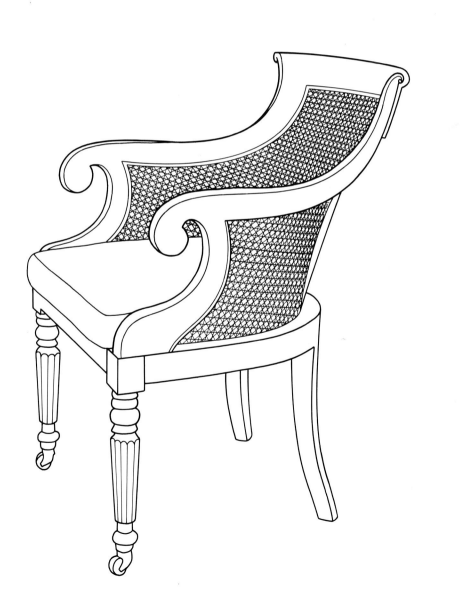

Victorian—
Nineteenth Century
1830-1900

In the Victorian age, the parade of styles broke loose into seemingly countless subformations. Designers aware of the history of style sought inspiration in the past. Some models were used as plain reactions against the familiar, but others were chosen for ideas suggested. The Gothic might be selected because it related to religion or to learning since great cathedrals and great universities were built in the Gothic style. The Rococo style was ideal for parlors because it was the style of fun-loving King Louis XV. Furniture in the Louis XVI and Renaissance Revival styles was more formal, and preferred for dining rooms.

In the period between about 1830 and 1870, designers tended to adapt historic styles with some care to retain the basic characteristics of the original. Although designs were free adaptations, they were easy to distinguish as the Gothic, Rococo, and Renaissance Revivals flourished. The simple, timeless country pieces that were made all through the 19th century include Shaker chairs which were produced at factories that flourished after 1860, although the designs relate to work of about 1800.

In the 1870s there was a radical change in the approach to design. Rather than adapting historic styles, chair designers devised innovative forms using a new choice of established motifs. One reason for the change was the dissatisfaction with much of the factory-produced historic revivals. Reformers pointed out the failures of designs executed with machine carving and cheap veneers. They advocated the use of simpler models that could be produced successfully by machine, or by craftsmen who could compete with the machine by making simple designs that would not take too much hand labor. The prime advocate of the change was Charles Eastlake whose book *Hints on Household Taste*, published in the United States in 1872, illustrated simple oak and cherry furniture. What is called Eastlake in American design is rectangular and simple, often made of oak or cherry, but sometimes ebonized or made of mahogany. The finest examples of American Eastlake design are products of the finest cabinetmaking shops in cities like New York, rather than the large mid-Western factories that had begun to flourish by the 1870s.

The Eastlake style was of importance in the 1880s and it was to be the beginning of a tradition that continued in the Arts and Crafts Movement. This movement called for a return to handwork and to simple forthright design. William Morris was a prime advocate, with the Arts and Crafts Exhibition Society in London getting under way in 1888. On the American scene the Eastlake, and then Arts and Crafts advocates, represented a strong trend opposed by the traditionalists.

Technological developments in the 19th century are not easy to understand. Patents for bending wood and for machinery to speed up production fill the listings of the Patent Office, but just how many were used before the 1880s is not easily determined. The most famous development, the bent and laminated wood used for Rococo Revival chairs, was a development that aided in the production of a design. It was, however, of no significance in simplifying production in general. Chair making required skilled hands as much at the end of the 19th century as it had at the beginning, and the factories were set up to speed production by having craftsmen concentrate on one phase of the job, like turning legs or carving backs. In factories or more traditional cabinetmaking shops, American chairs were as distinctive in the 19th century as they had been in the colonial era.

Transitional Victorian
1830-1850

Chair backs of the transitional Victorian period are as diverse in form as the Greek Revival houses they adorned. Whether they were factory made or the product of small shops, they shared a quality of restraint and refinement that mirrored an age when self-improvement societies, lyceums, and classical academies were popular.

Cyma-curved forelegs and a back that curves continuously down from the crest rail to the front of the seat rail are typical of many side chairs of the second quarter of the 19th century. Sometimes called a Gondola chair, the style is a continuation of American Empire, notably derived from the *klismos* chair, and represents the first significant Victorian style. Splats in lyre, straight, and vase shapes — with Rococo or Gothic details — are among the variations in side chairs (see above).

Materials: Transitional Victorian furniture was usually constructed of pine or other inexpensive woods and veneered with matched-grain mahogany. Between 1830 and 1850 new saws came into use that made it possible to produce veneers in much thinner and larger pieces.

Makers: Joseph Meeks and Sons of New York advertised such chairs as early as 1833. Francois Seignouret of New Orleans produced a Seignouret chair of gondola form with a vertical splat. Duncan Phyfe also produced handsome gondola chairs.

Gothic Revival
1830-1865

The detailing and decoration of Gothic Revival furniture, like that of Gothic Revival architecture, included not only Gothic arches, finials, crockets, and colonnets, but allusions to rose windows, as in the wheelback chair (right), which was designed by A. J. Davis in 1841 for the Gothic mansion on the Hudson now known as Lyndhurst. The chairs for which this preliminary study was made are still in the house.

This side chair with lancet arches and crockets was designed by architect Alexander Jackson Davis. Davis was a leader of the Gothic Revival in America, along with horticulturist and taste maker Andrew Jackson Downing. The chamfered moldings defining the Gothic tracery of the back, and the hoofed feet make this chair suggestive of later rustic furniture. High-backed side chairs were the most spectacular examples of the Gothic Revival style.

Materials: Rosewood, black walnut, and mahogany were the usual woods for Gothic Revival chairs, but Davis designed this one of oak.

Makers: This side chair may have been by Burns and Brothers, New York City, circa 1857. Davis's earlier furniture seems to have been made by Richard Byrne of White Plains, New York, and Ambrose Wright of Hastings, New York.

Louis XV Revival
1845-1870

By 1860 the balloon back had become the signature shape for its French-oriented age. Exposed-frame balloon-shaped backs appeared on upholstered and un-upholstered side chairs and armchairs.

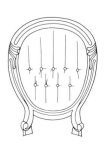

This rosewood armchair with floral motifs carved on its frame, cabriole front legs, and reverse-curve rear legs, typifies the Louis XV Revival. It was one of a set designed for the Colonel Robert J. Milligan house in Saratoga, New York. Deep-tufted upholstered seats and balloon-shaped backs are also characteristic of the style, as is naturalistic carving.

Materials: Black walnut and, occasionally, mahogany were used in addition to rosewood.

Makers: This chair was made by Galusha Brothers of Troy, New York, around 1855. Other major makers of Louis XV Revival chairs include A. Eliaers of Boston; Joseph Meeks and Sons of New York; George J. Henkels of Philadelphia; S. J. John of Cincinnati; and John Jelliff of Newark, New Jersey.

Rococo Revival —
John Henry Belter
1844-1863

The elaborate and intricate open carving of Belter's chairs would not have withstood normal wear had it not been for his laminating process. His method was to piece together layers of wood with the grain running at right angles, then to press the wood in steam molds to make it curve, and finally to pierce and carve it.

This typical Belter armchair has a laminated pierced-and-carved back comprising six to eight layers of veneer (see illustration above). Encircling the egg-shape tufted upholstered back of this Belter chair is pierced work in an oak-leaf pattern with an urn of flowers at the top. Elaborately carved cresting is in a floral-and-grape design above an ovolo molding in a scroll-and-cornucopia pattern. Finely executed carving in floral-and-grape motifs are continuously varied in Belter's work.

Materials: Belter chairs are always of laminated rosewood.

Makers: The work of the German-born John Henry Belter is a distinct variation on the Louis XV Revival style. Belter, who operated in New York City from about 1844 until his death in 1863, invented a laminating process, which he used in making the backs of his chairs and sofas. Charles A. Baudouine of New York was his most successful competitor.

Spool-turned Cottage
1850-1880

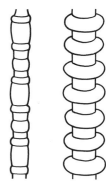

Some of the spool furniture of the 19th century came to be known as the Jenny Lind Style, because "the Swedish Nightingale" is supposed to have slept in a bed with spool turnings.

Spool-turned furniture was the first to be consistently factory manufactured and mass produced. It is characterized by continuously repeated bulbous turnings that suggest rows of spools. Today, spool beds are most familiar. This mahogany side chair has stiles, spindles, and front legs decorated with spool turnings. The pierced crest is composed of three whorls topped by heart shapes flanking a tear shape. The stiles end in urn-shaped finials. Four arches under the front rail have pointed drops suspended between them and a beaded band above.

Materials: Woods used for spool-turned chairs were black walnut, maple, birch, or other native hardwoods in addition to mahogany.

Makers: The manufacturer of this chair is not known, but it was produced in New York City around 1850. Spool-turned furniture was produced in many factories for the lower-priced market.

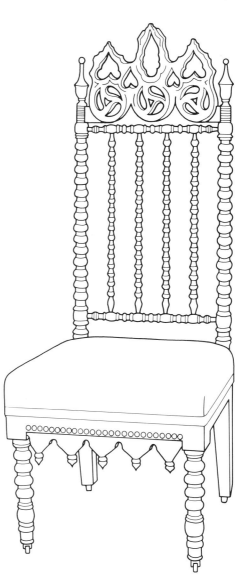

Eastlake Reform
1870-1890

Straight lines and incised decorations were recurring features of the Eastlake style, which admitted great variation, such as the incised foliate ornament (right) on the panel of a night stand made by Daniel Pabst.

In his influential *Hints on Household Taste* (1868), from which this low-back chair is one illustration, English architect and furniture reformer Charles Locke Eastlake recommended rectilinear forms, turned baluster-like supports and rows of spindles, shallow carving or inlaid ornamentation, and ebonized or dark-stained finishes. Eastlake advocated honest construction "without sham or pretense," feeling that machine carving should not look like hand carving. Americans avidly followed his precepts —if not always as he intended. His original drawing, therefore, is not typical of the heavier American models.

Materials: Black walnut, ash, cherry, maple, chestnut, and oak were used for American Eastlake pieces.

Makers: "Eastlake" chairs of questionable taste were designed and mass produced throughout the U.S., but they were also produced with competence and elegance by such craft shops as Herter Brothers in New York and Daniel Pabst in Philadelphia.

33

Turkish
1880-1890

The Turkish Bazaar at the 1876 Centennial Exhibition in Philadelphia helped inspire the many be-pillowed "Turkish cozy corners" and be-tasseled and be-tapestried chairs that appeared in American interiors in the 1880s.

Although far more comely than the "elegant Turkish", heftily upholstered and springed parlor furniture (above) offered in an 1897 Sears, Roebuck catalog, the draped tassels and tapestry seat of this side chair betray its exotic inspiration, which is overlaid on the Eastlake tradition. The true Turkish style, which was the predecessor of today's overstuffed furniture, also owed something to the popularity of Turkish rugs. In fact, embroidered tapestries, or fabrics woven in imitation of Turkish rugs, were generally used on Turkish chairs in conjunction with draped tassels and fringe.

Materials: Ebonized wood was used for this chair. Native hard and soft woods were used for upholstery-covered frames, black walnut or maple for turned legs.

Makers: Possibly made by Poitier and Stymus in New York around 1885 for the John Worshams, who were the previous owners of the John D. Rockefeller house in New York City, from which this chair was acquired by the Brooklyn Museum.

**Henry Hobson Richardson
1870-1886**

H. H. Richardson believed, as William Morris did, that "a true architectural work is a building duly provided with all necessary furniture."[2] The drawing (right) is a study for a chair for the Senate

Chamber in the New York State Capitol (1876-1881) designed by Richardson.

The overall simplicity of this armchair, with its turned spindles under the armrests, incised lines on the seat rail and handrests with carved animal heads, shows that H.H. Richardson designed furniture as monumental and straightforward as his Romanesque architecture. Richardson designed furniture only for his own buildings. While his designs may seem related to the furniture of his contemporary William Morris, and to the precepts of Eastlake, he created his furniture solely to harmonize with the library, church, or other public building for which it was intended.

Materials: Oak, as in almost all Richardson chairs.

Makers: Designed for the Crane Memorial Libreary in Quincy, Massachusetts (1880-1882), this chair, like many Richardson pieces, was executed by the A. H. Davenport company in Boston.

Shaker
1840-1910

The Illustrated Catalogue and Price List of Shaker Chairs *advertised furniture (right) manufactured by The Society of Shakers, in Mt. Lebanon, New York. It was first issued in 1874 by Elder Robert M. Wagan, who was responsible for the large factory built in 1873, where he installed modern machinery driven by steam.*

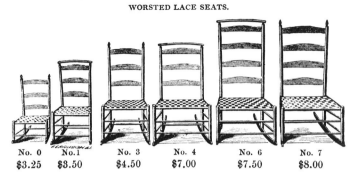

The Shakers' Slat Back Chairs, with Rockers.

WORSTED LACE SEATS.

No. 0	No.1	No. 3	No. 4	No. 6	No. 7
$3.25	$3.50	$4.50	$7.00	$7.50	$8.00

The plain tapered rear stiles of the slat back rocking chair are decorated with acorn finials. Vase shaped front stiles pierce the armrests, where they are topped by domed discs. The seat is of woven red and yellow cotton strips. The rockers, which have curved front ends, fit into slots in the bottom of the plain legs. Simple slat back chairs blend a classic, seemingly timeless directness of style and an honesty of construction into a singularly delicate appearance and distinctive scale; they are the most familiar Shaker furniture.

Materials: Stiles and stretchers of this chair are of birch; slats, arms, and rockers of soft maple. Many types of wood were used in the Shaker settlements scattered throughout the East and Midwest. The distinctive Shaker tape seat was an alternative to splint, rush, and cane seats. Tapes were originally handwoven of homegrown wool; later, cotton canvas was used.

Makers: The illustrated chair was made around 1875 in the Shaker settlement of Mt. Lebanon.

Adirondack
1870-1920

Usually made of twigs and branches with the bark left on, Adirondack chairs are nailed together in asymmetric patterns. The result is as far as anything could be from a machine-made chair. A symmetrical yet still rustic example is the bench (right) made of red cedar by the Rustic Construction Works, New York City, advertised in September 1919.

A notable contribution to American chairmaking appeared in the Adirondack wilderness of New York State toward the end of the 19th century. It was a chair built of twigs and branches, whose natural shapes dictated the way the pieces were joined. Although 18th century rustic garden furniture designs and 19th century factory-made garden chairs composed of realistic cast-iron "branches" had been known earlier, the rustic Adirondack chair probably owes less to that than to the 19th century cult of naturalism. The chair illustrated is one adorning the porch of Haag's Hotel in Shartlesville, Pennsylvania.

Materials: This chair (right) was made of tag alder around 1915. Other woods used include birch, hickory, beech, ash, wild cherry, or any suitable hardwood from nearby forests.

Makers: Commonly made by Adirondack carpenters, woodsmen, or guides, such chairs were also made in factories around New York City and in Indiana, then shipped to all parts of the country including the Adirondacks.

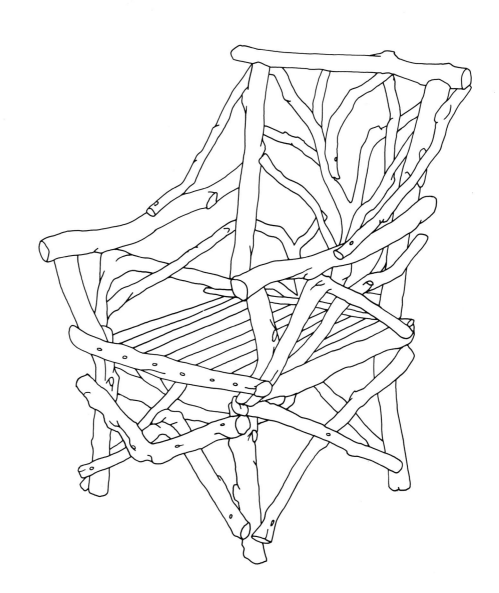

37

Twentieth Century—Modern
1900-1982

The wood chairs made in America have undergone more radical changes in the 20th century than in the previous three. What started in the 19th century as a rebellion against over-decorated design, has been developed into an approach to design that is the ultimate expression of 20th century American chairmakers. The basic challenge started by the Arts and Crafts Movement had questioned what could be executed successfully by machine, and the challengers had rallied for a return to handcraftsmanship. In this century designers resolved the problems by conceiving chairs that could be made by a combination of hand and machine production.

At the turn of the century Americans had gained an artistic self-confidence that made them capable of working in the fashionable international styles. Distinctive enough to be recognizable, the Americans captured the spirit of the advanced designs of the day. The plain craft-style chairs of Gustav Stickley's Mission furniture were as up-to-date as the Art Nouveau designs of Scottish architect Mackintosh. Frank Lloyd Wright's furniture was exhibited with the most innovative European work because it was simply another way of expressing the same concepts. In 1710 and in 1810 Americans were catching up with high fashion. By 1910, they were in the forefront, and as influential as they were influenced.

In the 1920s and the 1930s there were two major currents for modern design. One was the Art Deco, named for the international exhibition held in Paris in 1925. It involved the up-dating of traditional design. Fine cabinetmaking techniques were used for simple geometric interpretations of 18th and 19th century forms. The other, the Bauhaus style, is named for the German school that advocated a reevaluation of traditional forms and a development of new designs, some utilizing new materials other than wood. Americans were involved in work that reflected both tendencies, and by the forties there was some innovation in wood by revolutionaries like Charles Eames and Eero Saarinen who designed chairs of molded plywood.

Along with the new techniques there has been a trend to revive and support craftsmanship. Today there are small shops across the country where cabinetmakers are working like sculptors producing fine designs. At the same time factories do exist where handcrafted processes are enhanced by the use of modern technology. With renewed interest in the quality which results from the work of a human hand, there is hope in a future challenged by mass production. And while man-made materials fill essential needs in the production of seating—history teaches that there is something basic and essential in the craftsman/designer's expression through wood.

Mission Oak — Gustav Stickley 1901-1915

A detail (right), from one of the "Lessons in Craftsman Cabinet Work" in Craftsman *magazine, shows the mortise-and-tenon construction of a Morris chair like the one illustrated: "The tenons of the rails pass through the posts and project slightly, so that the manner of putting the piece together is both revealed and emphasized..."*[4]

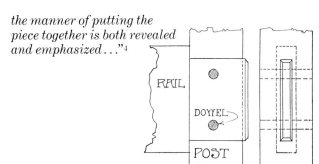

A sturdy and straightforward oak reclining chair is one of the first designs Stickley, advocate of the Mission style, patented in 1901. Horizontal or vertical slat backs are a feature of most Stickley chairs. Through his trade catalogs and *Craftsman* magazine, he familiarized countless readers with the Arts and Crafts Movement. The chair illustrated is clearly derived from the so-called Morris chair, which borrows its name from British poet-designer William Morris, chief spokesman for the Arts and Crafts ideal and champion of simple hand-crafted furniture loosely based on medieval forms.

Materials: "When I first began to use the severely plain, structural forms," Stickley wrote, "I chose oak as the wood that, above all others, was adapted to massive simplicity and construction."[3]

Makers: Stickley produced unadorned craft furniture in his Craftsmen Workshop in Eastwood, New York.

**Mission Oak—
Harvey Ellis
1903**

In addition to new models of furniture for Gustav Stickley, the versatile Harvey Ellis designed and illustrated houses and interiors that appeared in Stickley's Craftsman *magazine. The rendering (right) was one of his first to appear in the magazine in July 1903.*

Although similar to Gustav Stickley's Mission designs, this high-back oak armchair is distinguished by stylized inlays in its splats, by its elegant proportions, and by the gentle curve of its apron. In the 1890s the designs of architect-draftsman Harvey Ellis began to show inspiration from the British Arts and Crafts Movement. In 1903 he joined Stickley to contribute to *Craftsman* magazine and to design furniture. This is one of several pieces he designed for Stickley's Craftsman Workshops. Ellis's designs were accurately advertised as being "lighter in effect and more subtle in form than any former productions of the same workshops."[5]

Materials: Oak with inlays of pewter and copper. Ellis's inlays in various metals show an awareness of the work of C. R. Mackintosh and the Glasgow Group in Scotland.

Makers: Made in Stickley's Craftsman Workshops in Eastwood, New York, in 1903.

**Prairie School —
Frank Lloyd Wright
1904**

Spindle backs reaching from floor to crest rail were featured in many of Frank Lloyd Wright's early chairs, of which the Robie House dining chair (right) is a classic example.

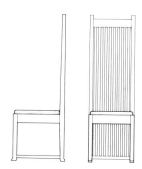

The circular and semicircular forms of the square-spindled oak barrel chair designed by Wright for the Darwin D. Martin house in Buffalo, New York (1904), represent a departure from his previous rectangular chairs; however, the back extending from floor to crest is characteristic. Whereas Wright's chairs changed, as his overall design style did throughout the decades, he repeated this design in the 1930s for the S. C. Johnson house in Racine, and also used it in his own home, Taliesin, in Spring Green, Wisconsin.

Materials: Wright's early chairs are of stained oak, but around 1910 he replaced the dark-stained furniture with unstained oak.

Makers: Matthews Brothers Furniture Co. in Milwaukee made Wright's Martin house furniture. Other early Wright furniture was made by the John W. Ayers Co. in Chicago, and the F. H. Bresler Co. of Milwaukee. This chair is in the collection of the Albright-Knox Museum, Buffalo.

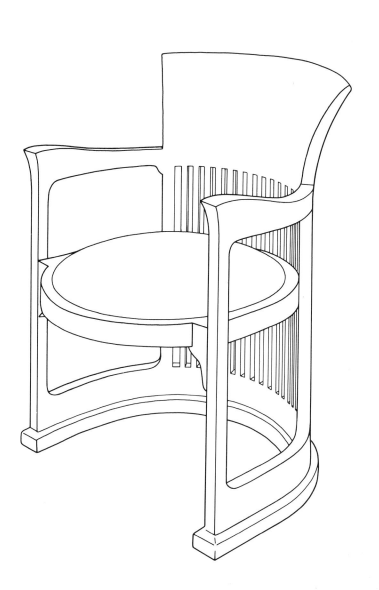

Arts and Crafts—
Greene and Greene
1907

The Greenes' philosophy of making "the whole as direct and simple as possible, but always with the beautiful in mind as the final goal,"[6] is evident in detailing. Sometimes they used square, highly polished ebony pegs to conceal screws and secure tenons in their furniture, but they also used them merely as decorative accents to set off the spartan qualities of their work.

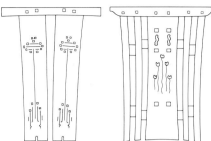

The delicate carving at the bottom of the legs, the ebony pegging, the ornamental apron brackets, and the gently rounded corners and edges of this mahogany armchair are typical of the detail found in the elegant furniture by California architects Charles and Henry Greene. Probably closer to the British Arts and Crafts Movement in their work than any other American designers of their time, the Greenes' special language was wood; they used it with superb craftsmanship in their houses, as well as in the furniture they designed for them. This chair, designed for the living room of the Robert R. Blacker house in Pasadena (1907), reflects the elements of oriental design that are evident in the house.

Materials: For their furniture the Greenes used walnut, teak, and fruitwood in addition to mahogany.

Makers: Construction of the Greenes' furniture was carried out by Peter Hall and craftsmen in his Pasadena workshop.

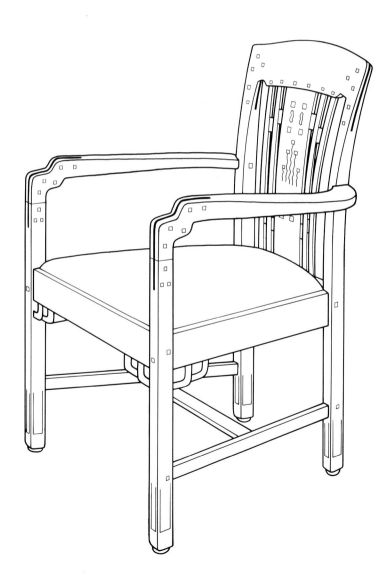

**Prairie School —
George Grant Elmslie
1909**

Elmslie's talents as an ornamentalist are apparent in the variety of his cutout designs for chair backs as well as in other elements of his interiors. An "idea for a chair" (right) is an Elmslie

drawing that specifies for its triangular splat: "Fabric with stencil or embroidery or flush inlay panel."

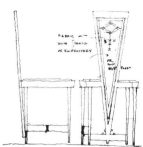

The richly ornamental geometric detail in the splat of this oak dining chair is reminiscent of the interweaving ornamentation devised by Louis Sullivan, in whose office Elmslie worked for many years. One of a set designed by Elmslie for his Charles A. Purcell house in River Forest, Illinois, the chair is ornamented by a tapering splat with cutouts in its laminated wood. As with most Prairie School architects, Elmslie's designs began with the simplicity of the Arts and Crafts Movement and were embellished with ornament in the Art Nouveau spirit. Other Elmslie dining chairs have similarly ornamented splats, the design motifs of which are carried out in such elements of his houses as rugs, fabrics and leaded glass.

Materials: Oak was the wood invariably used by Prairie School architects for their furniture.

Makers: It is possible, though undocumented, that Elmslie used the same shops as Frank Lloyd Wright to produce his furniture.

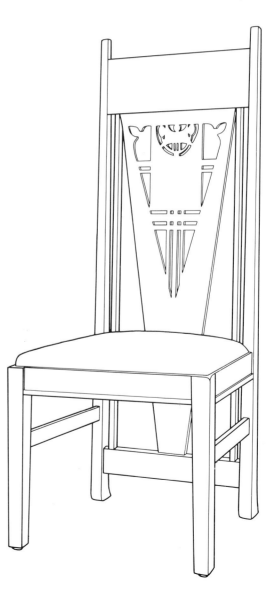

Art Deco — Eliel Saarinen
1930

The fine craftsmanship in the 18th century tradition that characterizes Art Deco furniture is evident in the chairs with fluted wood backs (right), designed by Eliel Saarinen, for his dining room at Cranbrook Academy of Art.

An elegant simplicity characterizes the dining chair designed by Finnish-American architect Eliel Saarinen for the president's house at Cranbrook Academy of Art in Bloomfield Hills, Michigan. It exemplifies the best of the Art Deco style, which flourished in the 1920s and 1930s. The gently flaring back suggests a fountain, a favorite symbol of the style, which attempted to achieve refinement through simplicity. The president's house (completed in 1929), in which Saarinen and his family lived, was one of the buildings he designed and equipped with furniture of his own design. The Art Deco movement in architecture and the decorative arts took its name from the 1925 Paris *L'Exposition Internationale des Arts Decoratifs et Industriels Moderne.* It has been described as an "assertive modern style" designed to adapt to mass production.

Materials: Holly wood inlaid with strips of ebony. The Art Deco style favored exotic wood.

Makers: Handcrafted at Cranbrook Academy of Art.

Modern —
Charles Eames
1946

Experiments with molded plywood by Charles Eames and Eero Saarinen helped give America a lead in technical innovations for furniture in the 1940s. Eames's famous molded plywood chair of 1946 will perhaps remain the epitome of the wood chair in the mid 20th century.

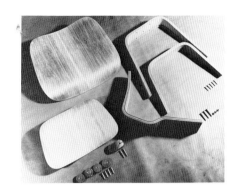

Considered one of the great chair designs of the post World War II Modern period, this molded bent plywood chair, with its pair of U-shaped plywood legs, is one of many versions designed by Charles Eames in 1946, to combine production-line methods with sensitive and "integral" design. The way the molded panels were bent in more than one direction was highly innovative, as was the rubber shockmount system, which attached the understructure to the back to give the chair resiliency. Other versions of what is now called "the Eames chair" have an understructure of steel rods instead of bent plywood.

Materials: Molded and bent birch plywood, rubber shockmounts. Ash and walnut were also used.

Makers: The Herman Miller Company began to produce Eames's chairs in 1949. This chair was manufactured in 1946 by the Evans Products Company, which for a short time produced the plywood for Eames's chairs.

**New Crafts—
Wharton Esherick
1956**

Originally a painter and sculptor, Esherick turned to furniture because, as he said, "I was impatient with the contemporary furniture being made—straight lines, sharp edges, and right angles—and I conceived free angles and free forms." [9] *The library lad-der (right) with its donkey and elephant finials is an eloquent example of his sculptural concepts and of his often humorous detailing.*

The sculptural quality of this chair, whose lines vaguely suggest a combination of Windsor, Morris, and Carver chairs, is typical of the furniture of Wharton Esherick—called the dean of 20th century American woodworkers. He is recognized as an influence on most of today's wood furniture craftsmen. Possibly influenced by Art Nouveau, Esherick's furniture has flowing organic forms that appeal to sight and touch. This chair, dating from 1956, follows a design he introduced in 1951.

Materials: Walnut and cherry with woven leather seat. Esherick used woods that were close at hand in his native Paoli, Pennsylvania. "If I can't make something beautiful out of what I find in my back yard, I had better not make anything," [7] he said.

Makers: At first Esherick worked by himself but later had helpers to do much of the joinery and finishing. In 1969, a year before his death, he was "still shaping the seats of the stools. The boys just don't get the hang of it." [8]

**New Crafts—
George Nakashima
1962**

Nakashima works "from the characteristics of the material and methods of construction outwards, to produce an integrated and honest object." [11] The walnut bench (right), with its slab seat formed from the trunk of a tree, juxtaposes polished natural graining with partly rough edges.

The design of the illustrated walnut chair by George Nakashima was first introduced in 1962. It suggests an Early American heritage in its spindle back and general simplicity, and is also evocative of traditional Japanese forms. Nakashima, who was born in Spokane, Washington, reveals the continuity of America's modern wood craftsmen in admitting that his designs may be related to Early American chairs because "in my work, too, I have tried to make an honest and simple use of wood." [10] Trained as an architect in the U.S., he went to Japan after graduation to work with architects, woodworkers, and carpenters. He returned to the U.S. in the 1940s and decided to go into furniture design because it was something in which he could maintain his standards of design and craftsmanship from beginning to end.

Materials: Figured walnut. Nakashima imports wood from all over the world.

Makers: At his workshop in New Hope, Pennsylvania, Nakashima's staff has grown to 12 workmen over the years.

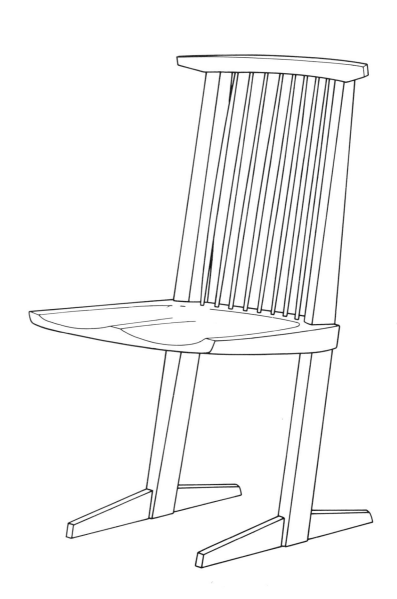

**Pull-Up Chair—
Ward Bennett
1965**

The simplicity and skeletal quality of Ward Bennett's round-carved chair reflects the designer's interest in exposed structural frames— exemplified in the architecture of Mies van der Rohe, and typified in the fluid lines of ancient Chinese chairs.

The chair, also produced with a cane seat and back, gives the appearance of a web-like transparent film within an exposed wood frame.

The flowing lines of this carved wood frame chair typify the sculptural quality found in many of Ward Bennett's designs. The crest rail flows into the arms and legs in one sweeping movement with no stretchers to interrupt the line. This is made possible by a three-dowel joint in the seat rail, rather than the usual one. Concealed dowel joints, sometimes complex, are typical in Bennett chairs, making them extremely strong, even when delicate in appearance. Referred to as the "skeleton" chair because of this exposed armature, it is both simple and comfortable—an excellent example of Bennett's concern with designing for the adult proportion.

Materials: The chair illustrated is of carved, natural oiled ash, with a French-upholstered back and tight seat. It is also produced in finishes varying from light to dark.

Maker: Brickel Associates Inc., New York.

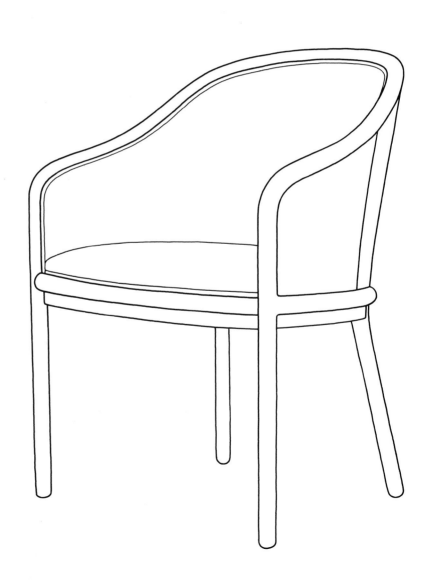

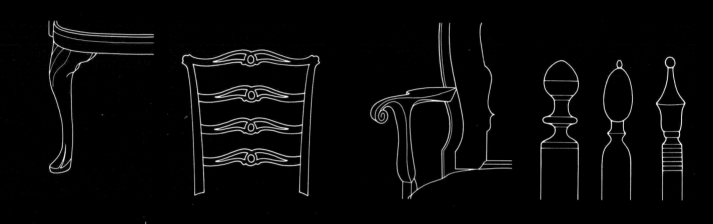

Glossary

1. *Arm*
2. *Arm support, or Front post*
3. *Back post, or Stile*
4. *Cross rail, Rung, or Slat*
5. *Finial*
6. *Foot*
7. *Handhold*
8. *Seat*
9. *Stretcher*
10. *Top rail*

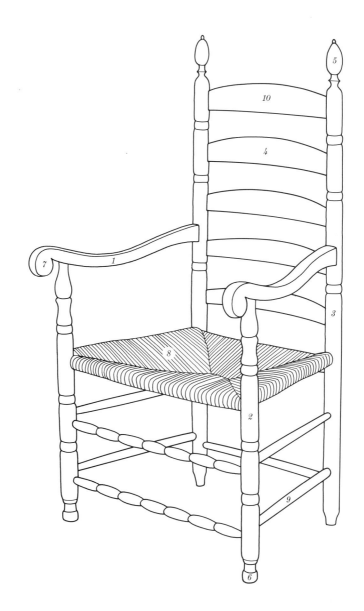

New England Slat Back

1. Apron, or Skirt
2. Arm
3. Back post, or Stile
4. Crest rail
5. Ear
6. Foot
7. Handhold
8. Knee
9. Leg
10. Seat
11. Seat rail
12. Splat

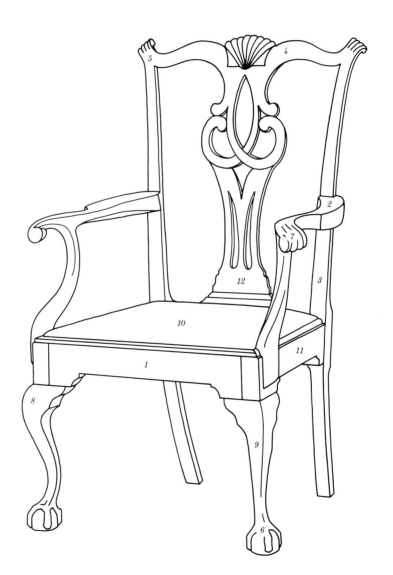

Connecticut Chippendale

Glossary

A

Acanthus

Conventionalized carved detail based on acanthus leaves; often used as decorative motif on knees of cabriole legs and crest rails of Queen Anne and Chippendale chairs. The acanthus leaf is the decorative motif of Corinthian capitals.

Adam, Robert

(1728-1792) Scots-born British architect whose Neoclassic interiors and furniture influenced Sheraton and Hepplewhite, and through them the design of American furniture during the Federal period.

Apron

Structural part of a chair directly beneath the seat. Also called a skirt.

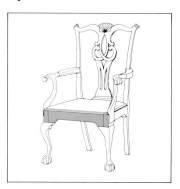

Connecticut Chippendale

Art Deco

Style of decoration popular in the 1920s and 1930s. It takes its name from the 1925 *Exposition Internationale des Arts Decoratifs et Industriels* in Paris. In contrast to the exuberant curves of Art Nouveau, Art Deco furniture is characterized by restrained forms, slender tapering legs, and the exploitation of exotic woods (see Eliel Saarinen chair, page 45).

Art Nouveau

Style originating as a reaction against Victorian eclecticism; lasting from 1885 to 1910. Its ornamental vocabulary is based on natural growing forms. The asymmetrically undulating line terminating in a whiplash movement is characteristic. It began in England in the 1880s but achieved its widest development in France and Belgium, where its influence on the decorative arts and architecture was apparent in the 1890s. The name derived from the shop, L'Art Nouveau, which Samuel Bing opened in Paris in 1895, and for which he commissioned painters and architects to design furniture and to decorate rooms.

Glossary

A-B

Arts and Crafts Movement

Renewal in the decorative arts that began in England in the 1860s and is usually associated with the activities of William Morris, who sought to revive the handcrafts in his increasingly mechanized age. In America, the Arts and Crafts Movement was evident in the Mission-style furniture of Gustav Stickley and the furniture of such architects as Frank Lloyd Wright, Charles and Henry Greene, and George Grant Elmslie.

Back

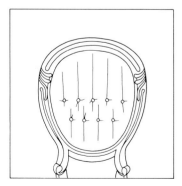

Balloon back
Exposed-frame chair back shaped like a balloon; often seen on side chairs and armchairs of the Louis XV Revival period (page 28).

Louis XV Revival

Back *continued*

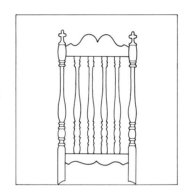

Banister back
Turned upright supports in chair backs. Sometimes called balusters (see William and Mary Banister Back, page 7).

William and Mary Banister Back

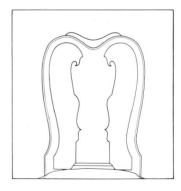

Fiddle back
Chair back with a single splat resembling the shape of a violin; often found on American Queen Anne chairs (see Queen Anne Fiddle Back, page 10).

Queen Anne Fiddle Back

B

Back *continued*

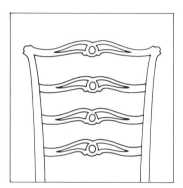

Ladder back
Chair back with horizontal rails or slats resembling a ladder; also called slat back (see Federal Ladder Back, page 16; New England Slat Back, page 9; Shaker, page 36).

Federal Ladder Back

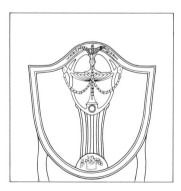

Shield back
Open chair back carved in the shape of a shield, a typical form used by Hepplewhite (see Hepplewhite Shield Back, page 17).

Hepplewhite Shield Back

Back *continued*

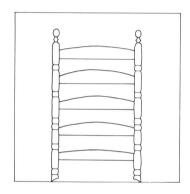

Slat back
(See Ladder back)

New England Slat Back

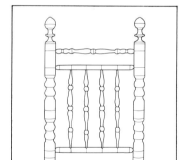

Spindle back
Chair back with slender upright supports — turned, round, or square (see Carver Spindle Back, page 5; Windsor Sack Back, page 13; Wright chair, page 42; Nakashima chair, page 48).

Carver Spindle Back

B

Back *continued*

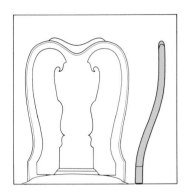

Queen Anne Fiddle Back

Spoon back
Chair back curved like a spoon in profile, conforming to the curvature of the spine (see Queen Anne Fiddle Back, page 10).

Sheraton Square Back

Square back
Open chair back in a square shape, a typical form used by Sheraton (see Sheraton Square Back, page 18).

Back *continued*

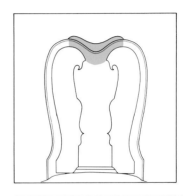

Queen Anne Fiddle Back

Yoke back
Chair back with a crest rail shaped like an ox yoke (see Queen Anne Fiddle Back, page 10).

Back Post

New England Slat Back

Rear outer uprights above a chair seat (see also Stile).

Glossary

Ball foot	(See Foot)	**Beading**	Decorative strip of molding that resembles small beads linked together.

Balloon back — (See Back)

Baluster — Turned or square upright support in chair back. Also called banister.

William and Mary Banister Back

Banding — Narrow strip of contrasting inlay, characteristic of furniture in the Federal period.

Banister back — (See Back)

Barrel chair — Chair shaped like a half barrel cut from top to bottom (see Frank Lloyd Wright chair, page 42).

Prairie School— Frank Lloyd Wright

Belter, John Henry — (1804-1863) German-born cabinetmaker and carver who worked in New York from 1844 until his death. The curved backs of his chairs and sofas were produced by a lamination process he developed to secure strength and permit carving. (See Rococo Revival — Belter chair, page 29.)

Bentwood — Wood that is bent into curves by water, steam, and pressure. A bentwood chair was patented by Samuel Gragg in the U.S. in 1808, and the process was further developed by Michael Thonet in Austria around 1840.

Block-and-vase turning — (See Turning)

Cabriole leg — (See Leg)

Glossary

C

Cane

Long narrow strips of rattan bark (a type of climbing palm) used to weave chair backs and seats (see William and Mary chair, page 8, and Late Empire — Zanzibar chair, page 23).

Chamfered

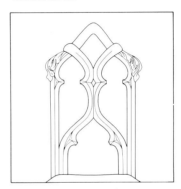

Gothic Revival — A.J. Davis

Beveled edge of a chair leg or molding; a square corner is cut off diagonally to make a chamfer.

Caryatid

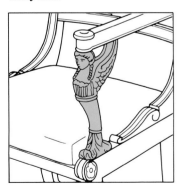

Greek architectural ornament in the form of a female figure; sometimes used as supports in Neoclassical furniture (see Empire — C.H. Lannuier chair, page 20).

Chippendale, Thomas

(1718-1779) English cabinet-maker whose book, *The Gentleman and Cabinet-Maker's Director*, first published in 1754, influenced American furniture makers of the 18th century and lent his name to a style of furniture (see Connecticut Chippendale chair, page 12).

Claw-and-ball foot

(See Foot)

C

Corner chair

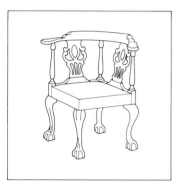

Chair with a seat set on a diagonal; usually with one leg in front, one in back, and one at each side. Sometimes called a roundabout chair (see Queen Anne Corner chair, page 11).

Crest rail

Top of a chair back.

Connecticut Chippendale

Crocket

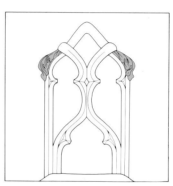

Gothic architectural ornament of conventionalized foliage; often occurring along the edges of a spire or finial.

Gothic Revival – A.J. Davis

Cromwell, Oliver

(1599-1658) Protector of England 1653-1658, whose name was given to the small Cromwellian chair that became popular in England during his protectorate and appeared in America in the late 17th century (see Cromwellian Leather, page 6).

Curule chair

Chair form based on an ancient Roman prototype with cross-base support and curved legs.

C-E

Cylix	Ornamental design based on Greek and Roman two-handled drinking cup set on stem and foot; most commonly used in the backs of Hepplewhite chairs of the Federal period (see Hepplewhite Shield Back, page 17).

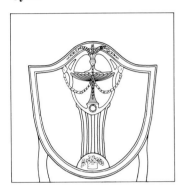

Hepplewhite Shield Back

Cyma curve	Double curve, half of which is concave, the other half convex; similar to the letter S, as in the front legs of the Transitional Victorian chair (page 26).

Transitional Victorian

Directoire	French Revolutionary period from 1799 to 1804, when classic Greco-Roman motifs came into favor. The Regency period in England took its inspiration from the same source.

Dog-paw foot	(See Foot)
Dowel	Cylindrical wood pin used to join two pieces of wood together.
Dowelled joint	Primary method used in joinery; a hole is cut at aligned points in two pieces of wood, which are then joined together by a wooden dowel.

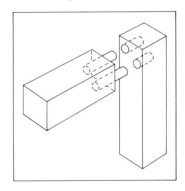

Ear	Extension of a crest rail beyond the back posts (see Connecticut Chippendale chair, page 12).

Connecticut Chippendale

E-F

Ebonized	Wood stained to resemble ebony, a black, finely-grained wood.
Eastlake, Charles Locke	(1836-1906) English author of *Hints on Household Taste* (1868), published in America in 1872, which propounded a philosophy of simplified and honestly constructed home furnishings and had a great influence on American furniture manufacturers in the 1870s and 1880s (see Eastlake Reform, page 33).
Fancy chair	Small decorative side chair based on Sheraton styles; usually painted, with a cane, rush, or plank seat (see Hitchcock chair, page 21).
Fiddle back	(See Back)
Fielded panel	A wood panel with beveled edges, set into a frame, creating a raised section or field (see Wainscot Panel Back chair, page 4).

Finial	Ornament decorating the terminal of a back post, often turned or carved in acorn (a), lemon (b), or urn (c) shapes.

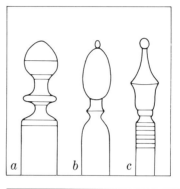

Fluting	Series of carved concave channels; the opposite of reeding. Fluted legs are characteristic of the Federal period (See Reeding).
Foot	**Ball foot** Large spherical turned foot.

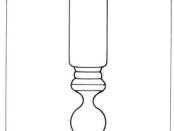

F

Foot *continued*

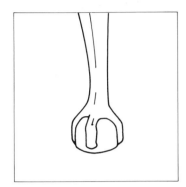

Claw-and-ball foot
An adaptation, allegedly from the Chinese, of a dragon's claw grasping a pearl; often terminating a cabriole leg of Queen Anne and Chippendale chairs. In America a bird's or eagle's claw is generally used (see Connecticut Chippendale chair, page 12).

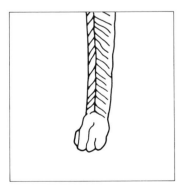

Dog-paw foot
Carved foot resembling the paw of a dog; similar to a lion's-paw. (See Duncan Phyfe chair, page 19).

Foot *continued*

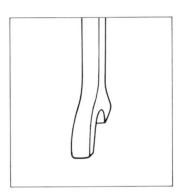

Hoofed foot
Carved foot resembling an animal hoof (see Gothic Revival chair, page 27).

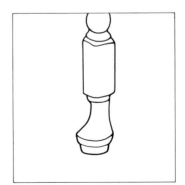

Pad-and-disc foot
Simple oval shape standing on a disc; usually terminating a cabriole leg but also used with block-and-vase turned legs, as in the Queen Anne Corner chair (page 11).

F-G

Foot *continued*

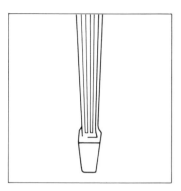

Spade foot
Rectangular foot resembling a spade at the end of a tapered leg (see Sheraton Square Back, page 18).

Spanish foot
Curved foot with carved scrolled toes usually terminating the legs of William and Mary chairs (see William and Mary Banister Back, page 7).

Gondola chair

Transitional Victorian

A chair with back posts curving continuously down to form the seat rail (see Transitional Victorian chair, page 26).

Gothic Revival
Style based on the medieval Gothic, which became popular in America between 1830 and 1865. Its first American proponents were landscape gardener Andrew Jackson Downing and architect Alexander Jackson Davis (see Gothic Revival chair, page 27).

Grain
Characteristic fiber patterns in different types of wood.

Greco-Roman
Style inspired by excavations at Herculaneum and Pompeii in the 18th century, which formed the basis for the furniture of the Federal and Neoclassical periods.

H-I

H-Stretcher

Typical chair stretcher construction in which horizontal rails join the front and back legs and are connected by a third stretcher in the middle to form an H.

Windsor Sack Back

Handhold

End of the chair arm where the hand usually rests.

New England Slat Back

Hardwoods

Wood of the broad-leaved trees such as oak, ash, maple, walnut, as contrasted with softwoods of the needle trees such as pine, spruce, hemlock. Hardwoods are generally used for unpainted furniture because of their close grain and durability.

Hepplewhite, George

(Died 1786) English cabinet-maker whose book, *The Cabinet-Maker and Upholsterer's Guide*, first published in 1788, was widely influential in America during the Federal period. Hepplewhite's designs were interpretations of Robert Adam's Neoclassic style (see Hepplewhite Shield Back, page 17).

Hitchcock, Lambert

(1795-1852) Connecticut chairmaker who began producing chair parts in 1818. He built a factory in 1825 to manufacture the "fancy" chairs based on Sheraton styles for which he became famous (see Hitchcock Fancy chair, page 21).

Inlay

Surface ornament formed by insetting wood or other material of contrasting color into a wood surface.

J-K

Jacobean

General term for the English styles made in the reign of James I (1603-1625) and sometimes that of James II (1685-1688). It is characterized by straightforward construction and simple outlines, generally bulky but often well proportioned. In America the term is sometimes applied to 17th-century Pilgrim furniture such as the Wainscot Panel Back (page 4); and the Carver Spindle Back (page 5).

Japanning

Process of covering furniture with paint, gesso, and varnish to simulate Oriental lacquering. Used in America throughout the 18th century.

Joiner

Woodworker who constructed furniture by framing members at right angles and fastening them together with mortise-and-tenon joints or wood dowels. Joinery is the oldest term for the craft of woodworking and furniture making.

Joint stool

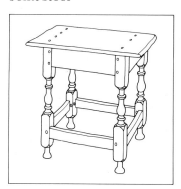

A simple backless seat with turned legs and stretchers. It was one of the earliest seating forms.

Klismos

Side chair used in ancient Greece. It had a concavely curved back and incurved saber legs, and served as a prototype for the Federal and Neoclassical periods (see Duncan Phyfe chair, page 19).

K-L

Knee

Outcurved, upper portion of a chair leg, as in the cabriole leg.

Connecticut Chippendale

Lacquer

Form of resinous varnish capable of taking a high polish; imported from the Orient to France early in the 18th century for its application to furniture (see Japanning).

Ladder back

(See Back)

Laminated

Building up layers of thin wood laid alternately across the grain for strength, a method used and refined by John Henry Belter (see Rococo Revival chair, page 29).

Lancet arch

Slender pointed Gothic arch sometimes used in chair backs during the Gothic Revival period.

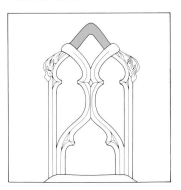

Lathe

Machine used for shaping wood (see Turning).

Leg

Cabriole leg
Curving chair leg that generally follows an inverted S-form; with outcurved knee and incurved ankle, used on Queen Anne and Chippendale chairs.

L

Leg *continued*

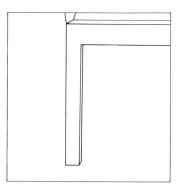

Marlborough leg
Straight leg often terminating in a simple block-shaped foot. Most commonly used on chairs in the Chippendale style and less frequently on chairs of the American Sheraton period (see Federal Ladder Back chair, page 16).

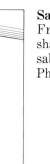

Saber leg
Front leg of a chair with a sharp curve like that of a saber; often found on Duncan Phyfe chairs (page 19).

Leg *continued*

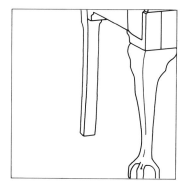

Stump leg
Simple thick leg most commonly used for the rear legs of Chippendale and Queen Anne chairs (see Connecticut Chippendale, page 12 and Queen Anne Fiddle Back, page 10).

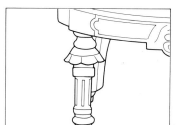

Trumpet leg
Turned leg resembling an upturned trumpet; sometimes used on Renaissance Revival chairs (page 31).

L-M

Lyre

Naturalistic representation of the Greek lyre. As a furniture ornament the form was introduced to England from France by Robert Adam and reached America in the Federal period. It was often used in chair backs by Duncan Phyfe and Charles Honoré-Lannuier (see pages 19 and 20).

Louis XV

King of France 1715-1774. The period was marked by the flowing S-curve lines of the Rococo style (see Louis XV Revival, page 28, and Rococo Revival—Belter, page 29).

Louis XVI

King of France 1774-1793. His period produced the Neoclassical style based on the straight and rectangular lines of ancient classicism (see Louis XVI Revival, page 32).

Marlborough leg

(See Leg)

Mission

Style of sturdy oak furniture with its source in the Arts and Crafts Movement; achieved wide popularity between 1900 and 1916. The best known Mission furniture was produced by Gustav Stickley in his Craftsman Workshops in Eastwood, New York, but two of his brothers, Leopold and J. George Stickley, also produced Mission furniture in Fayetteville, New York, as did Elbert Hubbard at his Roycroft Shops in East Aurora, New York.

McIntire, Samuel

(1757-1811) Architect, carver, and furniture maker in Salem, Massachusetts, during the early Federal period.

Morris, William

(1834-1896) English artist, architect, poet, and leader of the Arts and Crafts Movement. Morris, Marshall, Faulkner & Company, the decorative arts firm he established in 1861, was influential in America as well as in England.

M-P

Mortise and Tenon

Method of joinery wherein a rectangular hole or slot cut into a piece of wood (mortise) is joined to a tongue (tenon) projecting from another piece of wood.

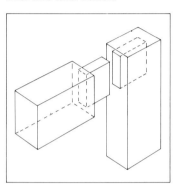

Ormolu

Gilded bronze decoration on French 18th-century furniture; also used by American furniture makers early in the 19th century (see Empire — C.H. Lannuier chair, page 20).

Ovolo

Rounded convex classical molding, usually the quarter of a circle. It was often used by John Henry Belter in the carved detail of his chairs (see page 29).

Pad-and-disc foot

(See Foot)

Patina

Rich surface appearance of wood resulting from polishing and age.

Peg

Another term for a wood pin or dowel used to join two pieces of wood together. The term peg usually implies a pin or dowel, the head of which is exposed.

Phyfe, Duncan

(1768-1854) Scots-born cabinetmaker who worked in New York City from about 1795 to 1847, and whose career encompassed the entire Federal — Neo-classical periods.

P

Pierced splat

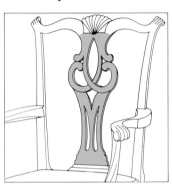

Back splat of a chair with carved openwork; usually done with a fret saw (see Connecticut Chippendale chair, page 12).

Plank seat

Windsor Sack Back

A solid wood chair seat such as the seat of a Windsor chair (see page 13).

Plywood

Several thicknesses or plies of wood glued together so that the grain of any one ply is at right angles to the grain of adjacent ply; a laminating process patented in the U.S. in 1865. Plywood molded in two directions was the 20th-century furniture innovation of Eero Saarinen and Charles Eames (see page 46).

Prairie School

Group of architects led by Frank Lloyd Wright in the early 20th century. With his Midwest contemporaries, Wright developed a style of architecture characterized by the horizontal lines of the prairie. Many of the Prairie School architects designed simple furniture for their Prairie houses based on the ideas of the Arts and Crafts Movement (see Frank Lloyd Wright chair, page 42; and George Grant Elmslie chair, page 44).

P-R

Prince of Wales feathers

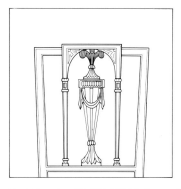

Sheraton Square Back

Decorative motif of three ostrich feathers (symbol of the Prince of Wales) used in chair backs during the Sheraton-Hepplewhite period (see Sheraton Square Back, page 18).

Ram's horn arm

Arm support shaped somewhat like a ram's horn (see William and Mary Banister Back, page 7).

Queen Anne

Queen of Britain 1702-1714, who gave her name to the furniture style during her reign. It reached America in the 1720s (see Queen Anne Fiddle Back, page 10 and Queen Anne Corner chair, page 11).

Rail

Horizontal member of wood, usually joining vertical posts; such as the crest rail or stretchers of a chair.

Reeding

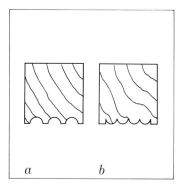

Series of convex vertical channels; the opposite of fluting (a). Reeded legs (b) are characteristic of chairs in the Sheraton style (see Sheraton Square Back, page 18).

Glossary

Regency

English period roughly 1793-1820, before and during which the Prince of Wales, later George IV, acted as Regent. The furniture style of the period was influenced by excavations in Herculaneum and Pompeii. It was interpreted later in America by Duncan Phyfe and Charles Honoré-Lannuier.

Renaissance Revival

Eclectic furniture style of the Victorian period roughly based on the 16th-century French Renaissance designs. It is characterized by heavy proportions and elaborate decoration often inspired by architecture rather than furniture design (see Renaissance Revival chair, page 31).

Ring turning

(See Turning)

Ring-and-ball-turning

(See Turning)

Rococo

A style of architecture and ornamentation chiefly developed during the reigns of Louis XIV and Louis XV. It was characterized by asymmetrical natural forms such as rocks and shells.

Rung

(See Stretcher)

Rush seat

A chair seat woven of rushes, a type of plant with cylindrical stems. Used in America from earliest times, generally with simple furniture.

New England Slat Back

Saber leg

(See Leg)

Saddle seat

A wood seat that is cut away from a center ridge in a downward slope to the sides; somewhat resembling the seat of a saddle; commonly found on Windsor chairs.

Windsor Comb Back

Sausage turning

(See Turning)

S

Scroll arm

Chair arm that terminates in a scroll in front. (see Late Empire — Zanzibar chair, page 23).

Serpentine arm

Undulating chair arm (see Connecticut Chippendale chair, page 12; and Hepplewhite Shield Back, page 17).

Seat rail

The part of a chair frame on which the seat is constructed or rests.

Connecticut Chippendale

Sheraton, Thomas

(1751-1806) English cabinet-maker whose book, *The Cabinet-Maker and Upholsterer's Drawing-Book*, published in 1791-1794, was widely influential in America during the Federal period. Sheraton's designs, like those of Hepplewhite, were interpretations of Robert Adam's Neoclassic style (see Sheraton Square Back, page 18).

Shield back

(See Back)

S

Skirt	(See Apron)
Slat back	(See Back)
Slip seat	Removable upholstered seat that fits inside a seat frame.
Softwoods	Wood of such needle trees as pine, spruce, hemlock, commonly used for painted furniture (see Hardwoods).
Spade foot	(See Foot)
Spanish foot	(See Foot)
Spindle	A rod or pin — sometimes tapered, sometimes turned — used in the structure or decoration of chair backs.

Carver Spindle Back

Spiral turning	(See Turning)

Splat	Broad, flat upright support in the middle of a chair back.

Queen Anne Fiddle Back

Splint seat	Chair seat made of thin interwoven strips of oak or hickory; commonly used in country furniture throughout the 18th century.
Split baluster	Turned upright support in a chair back that has been split so it is half round (see William and Mary Banister Back, page 7).
Spool turning	(See Turning)
Spoon back	(See Back)
Square back	(See Back)

S-T

Stile

Connecticut Chippendale

One of the two rear, outer vertical side supports in the frame of a chair, reaching from crest rail to foot (see also Back Post).

Stop fluting

A style of fluting in which the lower part of the carved channels are filled with reeding; most often found in a chair leg.

Stretcher

New England Slat Back

Horizontal crosspiece that connects chair legs, adding strength and support; used in a variety of configurations (see H-Stretcher and X-Stretcher).

Stump leg   (See Leg)

Tape seat

Chair seat made of interwoven strips of cotton tape; commonly used on simple country chairs (see Shaker chair, page 36).

Trumpet leg   (See Leg)

Turner

Woodworker who shapes furniture parts — such as legs, balusters, and spindles — by turning them on a lathe.

T-W

Turning

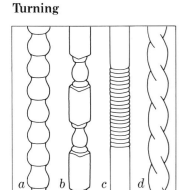

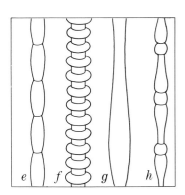

The shapes produced by turning wood pieces on a lathe. Among the many types are:

Ball
(a) Spherical shapes (see Carver Spindle Back chair, page 5).

Block-and-vase
(b) Combination of square and urn shapes (see Queen Anne Corner chair, page 11, and William and Mary Banister Back, page 7).

Ring
(c) See Hitchcock — Fancy chair, page 21 and New England Slat Back, page 9.

Spiral
(d) Rope-like twists (see Cromwellian chair, page 6).

Sausage
(e) See Queen Anne Corner chair, page 11.

Spool
(f) See Spool-turned Cottage chair, page 30.

Vase
(g) See Windsor Sack Back, page 13.

Vase-and-ball
(h) See Carver Spindle Back, page 5.

Urn-shaped finial	(See Finial)
Vase turning	(See Turning)
Vase-and-ball turning	(See Turning)
Veneer	Thin layer of fine wood glued onto a base wood for decorative effects of grain.
Victorian	General term for English and American furniture produced during Queen Victoria's reign, 1837-1901.
Water-leaf carving	Carved ornamental detail of a narrow leaf with regular undulations divided by a central stem. A classical motif often used by Duncan Phyfe and Charles Honoré-Lannuier as a leg decoration (see Empire — C.H. Lannuier chair, page 20).
William and Mary	King and Queen of England 1689-1702, who gave their names to the furniture style that prevailed in the English-speaking colonies from 1690 to 1730 (see William and Mary Banister Back, page 7 and William and Mary chair, page 8).

W

Windsor chair

Spindle-back chair made from bending and shaping green wood. Spindles and legs are socketed into a solid wood seat. Among the main types are:

Bow Back
The continuous steam-bent crest rail is shaped like a bow (or hoop) and mortised into the seat. If an armchair, the arms are mortised into the bow.

Comb Back
Chair back resembles a comb, usually found in arm-chairs.

Windsor chair *continued*

Continuous Arm
Steam-bent crest rail curves down to form the arms.

Fan Back
Resembles the comb back but the spindles fan out.

W-X

Windsor chair *continued*

Low Back
Short spindles of about the same length are topped by crest and arm rails making a continuous curve. This was the inspiration for the popular Captain's chair.

Sack Back
Bow-like crest rail is mortised into an arm rail. Back spindles extend from crest rail through arm rail into seat (see Windsor Sack Back, page 13).

Windsor chair *continued*

Writing Arm
Arm is enlarged to form a writing tablet.

X-Stretcher
Stretcher construction in which X-shaped horizontal rails join the front and back legs.

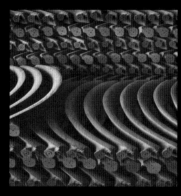

o

5

Ward Bennett on Designing

It is the volume that concerns me, the inside and the outside as they contain and support the human form. Like the ceramic tea bowl of oriental tradition, as the ancient Chinese philosopher Lao Tzu has said, "A clay bowl is molded, but the use of the bowl depends on the part of the bowl that is void."

Today, whether making sculpture, designing space, or designing a chair, it is my desire to make the form, the space, as meaningful and poetic as possible. Chairs are especially important to me. Chairs are sculpture. Brancusi, whom I had the privilege of knowing, inspired me as a young man. To whatever subject he directed his considerable talents—sculpture or the design of furniture—he always captured the essence, the simplest form.

But even as they are sculpture, chairs must, first and foremost, support the human frame. They are challenging because to be beautiful they must be functional. Things that cannot be used possess something negative, even if beautiful. Real beauty asks to be used.

And while basic proportions are considered, the variety of human *movement* that a chair permits and facilitates must

Ward Bennett in his Scissor chair.

In my chair design, after I have studied the positive and negative spaces, I sculpt the membrane that exists between man and space. The form must support man and allow movement within it. But it is the integrity and relationship between the inside and the outside that create the beauty that is found in nature.

also be considered. A chair must satisfy the need to stretch, to throw one's leg over the arm, to sit erect and attentive. Then—since we have different requirements for work chairs, lounge chairs, and dining chairs—a chair must be proportioned to its intended purpose.

Today there are more chairs than there have ever been before—millions and millions, including seats in cars, subways, railroads, and airplanes. And the majority of them really are not functional. Our sedentary society is increasingly a victim of poor chair design resulting in an ever-increasing number of spinal and lower lumbar disfunctions, and permanent disabilities. An excellent doctor taught me about my own needs for proper lumbar support—the physical realities of sitting.

The first step in designing a chair, is to establish the pitch. I start with an old or new chair that I find particularly comfortable—either someone else's or my own.

Ward Bennett
on Designing

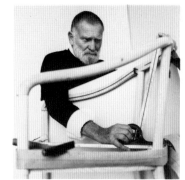

All I am interested in is the seat and lower back section, at this stage. So I eliminate the arms, legs, and upper portion of the chair, then attach the seat to a box or bench.

In designing a chair, or any other piece of furniture or object, the adult human proportion is my prime concern. A person should be able to sit *in* a chair — not just *on* a chair. This means that the pitch of the seat — its angle in relation to the back — is of crucial importance (see photograph, top right). The height from seat to floor and the height and shape of the arms are much more than design elements — they are critical anatomical concerns.

From this start I create an armature while sitting in the chair — using flexible materials such as reed or bamboo, wire, cardboard, and stretch fabric. I make shapes relating to arm height, shoulder and back support.

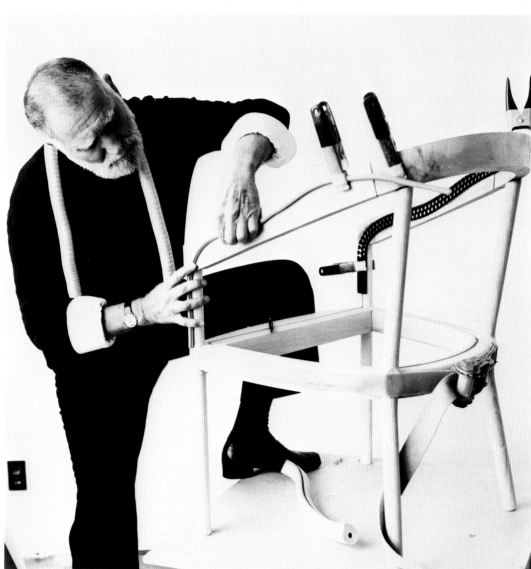

Creating the shape of an arm.

Having worked in stone, metal, glass, leather, and wood —my goal is to understand the essence of each material; to comprehend its inner strength; to respect its organic integrity. And, it is to understand well a utilitarian object's intended purpose. For it will be truly beautiful only as it is truly useful.

A chair is made to support the adult human frame as a seashell supports a snail or a pea pod supports a pea. The shape of a chair should be determined by the mass it is intended to support. The very rationale for its existence is its response to this necessity.

Once I build this kind of model, I work with the pattern maker to create the templates that will result in an actual finished chair. And it is then, in the manufacturing process, that the chair comes to life, as the craftsman works the materials, sculpting and carving them, to make what is still virtually a handmade artifact.

Testing the prototype for comfort.

Receiving/Stock Cutting

Choice raw lumber is kiln dried and scientifically seasoned to control shrinking, swelling, warping, or splitting. Thus prepared, these woods can be machined with precision, fastened and glued properly, and finished with the best results.

Boards can be cut from a log in several patterns, depending on what the wood will be used for and how much waste can be permitted. Four ways of cutting a log into planks are shown in this diagram from Masonry Carpentry Joinery, *Scranton, 1899.*

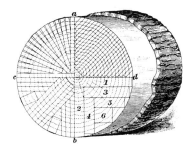

The production of chairs of Brickel Associates' quality begins with the initial choice of lumber and drying process. Green lumber fresh from the forest is nearly impossible to work with because it is full of sap and stringy fibers. In earlier times air drying was the only curing method; it could take as many as seven years to season wood properly. Today, kiln drying has considerably sped the process of curing wood, and has eliminated the irregularities that occur in wood that has been exposed to changing weather conditions.

Lumber, arriving by the truckload, is received by the stock-cutter, whose inspection of the wood constitutes the first phase of production and quality control.

The stock-cutter verifies that the wood is only "First Grade" lumber, inspects carefully for the smallest defects —knots, stains, or splits— that might impair the quality of the finished product. Such

Stock-cutter sawing boards into blocks.

imperfections will be cut out when the wood is "rough cut" to blocks of appropriate size for each group of chair parts.

In laying out his rough cut pattern, the stock-cutter chooses the sections of lumber that will best accommodate each chair part, both in terms of grain and structural strength. He lays his templates to achieve the least amount of waste and the most efficient use of labor. At the same time, he plans his rough cuts so any defective areas of wood can be discarded. And he must place the templates so that each finished chair part will be cut from a single block of wood. In Ward Bennett chairs, no glued joints from pieces of wood glued edge to edge are visible to impair the aesthetics of the finished chair.

When stock-cutters have produced a maximum yield of first quality cuts from each shipment of First Grade hardwood, the rough cut wood passes into the second major phase of production.

Tracing the template.

Machine Cutting

Some of the cut pieces require no further shaping and will pass directly to the sanding process.

Some wood parts are cut and carved; others are cut only. Flat pieces that are not carved are most always covered by upholstery.

Before the final shaping of the wood is done in multiples, a complete prototype chair is assembled using the new wood marked against the pattern. This prototype serves to verify that all the parts have been properly traced and cut, that they will interlock as tightly as possible. This ensures a sturdy and durable product, and also avoids large scale errors in terms of poorly cut or faultily aligned parts that might have to be discarded.

Machine cutting the wood to shape on a bandsaw.

Other chair parts require more intricate shaping; these cut pieces will next be carved on a multiple spindle machine.

Once this initial check has been made, the rough cut lumber is ready to be cut or carved, depending on the desired shape. Flat pieces are machine cut on a bandsaw. Continuous curves, broken lines with sharp corners and other difficult cuts may be made on a bandsaw, a profiler or a shaper.

To operate a bandsaw it is customary first to mark the line to cut on each piece of wood. This is generally done against the edge of a pattern. The operator then lays the marked piece on the table and feeds it into the bandsaw by hand. Accurate bandsawing requires considerable skill and experience.

Machine cutting blocks of wood, which will later be machine carved.

Machine Carving

Progression of a chair part: The wood block is cut to the shape traced with the template. The cut piece is carved to match the metal die (second from top). Top — the carved piece.

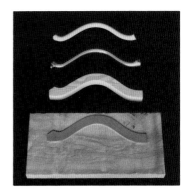

Sculptural pieces are machine carved. The modern technology of multiple spindle machinery has sped up the cutting and carving process considerably. With as many as 24 spindles on a machine, chair parts can be produced in lots of 24 at a time. However, since every spindle is guided by the experienced hand of the machinist, the process is still essentially a handcrafting method.

In this phase, machine cut blocks of wood are positioned and clamped on the spindle machine, each with a cutting or carving tool in the spindle poised above it. A variety of cutting tips are used to obtain a specific shape such as round, flat, or bevelled.

At the center of the machine the master spindle holds a tracer point, beneath which an aluminum die of the desired chair part is clamped in place. The machinist moves the tracer across the die gently and carefully, following every line, curve, and

Multiple spindle carving machine.

The small holes shown at the ends of these carved chair parts were carefully made before carving to position the wood securely on the multiple spindle machine.

groove. As he moves the tracer, the spindles to the right and left move identically. When he has covered the entire face of the die, each cutter will have trimmed its wood block to the same size and shape.

The pace at which the machinist works and the fluidity of movement as he traces the metal die is reiterated by every spindle, and visible in every piece of wood. If he moves too quickly, or if his cutting tools are dull, the surface of the cut will be rougher than desired, and sanding time will be increased. Since sanding even a smooth cut is a time-consuming job, it is worth the extra effort to cut or carve as smoothly as possible.

As each piece is unloaded from the spindle machine, it is again inspected for imperfections or weak points. With the strict quality control prior to cutting, an imperfect chair part is rarely found at this point.

The hand of the machinist guides the master spindle.

Precision Boring

The illustration of a dowelled joint (right) from Masonry Carpentry, Joinery, *Scranton, 1899, instructs "The holes should be somewhat deeper than the length of the dowels, to allow for shrinkage of the material and at the same time insure a close joint."*[12]

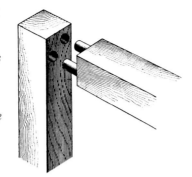

The alignment of chair parts and the strength of interlocking structure depend critically on the boring of holes for concealed dowels and screws. It is especially important to Brickel chairs, which are made with sophisticated dowel joinery.

A machinist achieves utmost precision by clamping the stock immovably in place, by using pressurized air to remove all chips from the wood surface, and by using multiple spindle machines for exact spacing of several holes at a time.

Some boring machines hold the stock stationary while the cutterheads move against it; in other machines the wood is brought against the cutterheads. Some clamps are equipped with air pressure to cushion the wood from vibration due to drilling.

The creation of a perfectly matched dowelled joint requires an expert understanding of wood technology.

Rough Sanding

Drum sanders rotate at various speeds and remove imperfections from the raw furniture parts. Beltsanders are driven by a cylinder; they enable a machinist to sand a large flat surface to a precise thickness. Some of the machines require two craftsmen at a time to sand one piece of wood.

To this point all the processes have been performed by cutterheads revolving at high speeds, gouging the wood. Now, the chair parts must be sanded. This is the first of several stages of sanding that bring out the essential beauty of a quality chair with fine exposed wood. Some parts, if they are curved or shaped, may require extensive hand-sanding. As many as six hours total sanding, performed throughout the manufacturing process, may go into one chair.

Rough sanding is the first stage. Craftsmen begin with coarse sandpaper, then gradually shift to finer grades. Most rough sanding is done with small, power-driven sanders that can be hand-held and manipulated around the shaped pieces of wood.

Sanding the unassembled chair parts on a beltsander.

Gluing and Assembling

All parts of the chair prior to assembly: back post, arms, stiles, seat rails, apron, front legs. Chair is joined entirely with dowelled joints and glue.

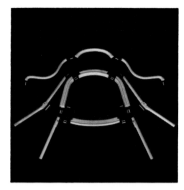

Chairs such as those designed by Ward Bennett, which have hidden joint construction, must be assembled —like a puzzle—in a specific order, or the parts will not fit together.

In addition to design concerns, scientific principles of stress have been studied to determine how and where to place the dowel joints. At each joint, the entire surface of the dowel must perform its job of gripping and absorbing stress. Maximum strength is built into these concealed joints by coating each surface of the dowel and each cut end of wood thickly and evenly with the adhesive. Leaving even a fraction of the dowel surface uncoated with glue would result in a weakened chair construction.

Placing dowels into position in the bored holes.

This cross-section of a seat rail and stile shows complicated joinery, which bolsters the chair's seat rail at a stress point.

Not only must the glued joints have sufficient strength—both shear strength and tension strength—they must not lose their strength with age. Resistance to moisture, chemicals, heat, fungus, and mold is a major requirement of glue. In addition it must take the stain and finishing materials.

There are various types of glue including animal glue, once used exclusively by craftsmen; casein glue, one of the early water resistant products; soy bean glue, generally used for plywood. Polyvinyl glue, the glue used in the manufacturing of Brickel chairs, came into use during World War II when it was difficult to get animal glue. It works at room temperature (about 60°-90°F) and generally takes only about half an hour to cure. It is strong, and has good pot life.

Glued ends of a dowelled joint are aligned.

Gluing and Assembling

An "exploded" chair shows its concealed dowel joinery.

Chairs are glued and assembled in parts, from the bottom upward. Clamping, which is the other half of the gluing process, is carefully performed to assure maximum adhesion of the glue. A system of metal clamps is affixed to press the parts together tightly without marring the sanded surface of the wood.

The clamps create enough pressure to squeeze all the excess glue out of each joint. Once dried, this excess will be removed in final sanding stages. Correct pressure is important. If it is not enough, there will be weak joints in the chair; if it is too much, the film of glue may be squeezed so thin that weak joints result. There is, however, more danger in too little than too much pressure.

Chairs are tightly clamped wherever glue has been applied.

The glued and assembled chairs, tightly clamped, are left to cure.

Pressure is not so critical in edge gluing. In joint gluing it is not the pressure of clamps that determines pressure on the glue line, it is proper fit to ensure wood-to-wood contact when the joint is assembled that is important. In edge gluing, the pressure of the clamp is what gives wood-to-wood contact in the joint. An important function of pressure is to keep the glued parts from moving while the glue is curing.

Once clamped, the fully assembled chair is left to cure until completely dry. Then it is taken to the levelling table where the chair legs are adjusted to be perfectly even. Now the chair is ready for the final sanding and finishing processes.

The fully assembled chair is clamped at every stress point.

Fine Sanding

The finest grades of sandpaper, hand-applied, smooth out every groove, joint, and curve of the assembled chair. Even the underneath parts, which do not normally show, are sanded.

In the final stages, sanding serves a double function. It removes the excess glue from the joints, and also smoothes out every last flaw in the wood so that the individual chair parts flow into each other in uninterrupted lines of design and wood grain.

At this stage of sanding when the finest grades of paper are used, the craftsman will often put aside his tools and finish the process with hand-sanding. He will frequently run his hands over the wood to judge texture and check uniformity of surface.

When the parts of a chair are mostly carved rather than being cut into large flat pieces, the sanding operator has final command over the shape of each chair. Although a line of chairs may have identical dimensions, no two are exactly alike.

At this stage, the assembled chair frames are in their rawest state.

Caning

The centuries-old art of caning appeared in America late in the 17th century after it had been introduced into England several years earlier. The trade of the East India Companies had made Oriental caning familiar and by 1680 the making of cane chairs was a specialized industry in England, where apprentices split imported Indian canes and skilled frame makers completed the product. Cane is made from the outside bark of the rattan, a climbing palm of the jungles. It is imported from the Far East and woven in various cross-patterns (see illustration above).

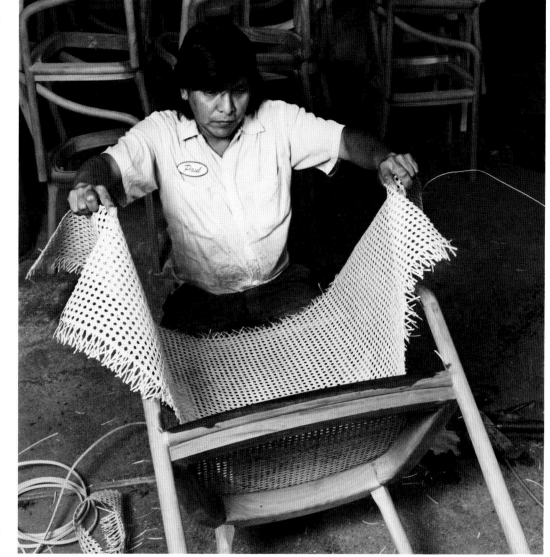

A single piece of caning is used for this chair's back and arms.

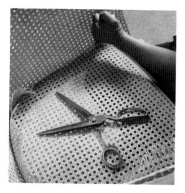

Before use, the caning is soaked in water to render it flexible. As the damp caning dries, it will contract slightly, creating a properly taut fit.

Today raw caning comes to the workshop in rolls. A piece of caning is cut to shape with a margin of overlap, and placed over the seat or back. A chair that has been manufactured to accept caning on its seat or back will have a groove—a router line—cut into the frame. The cane is hammered into the router line and secured with glue. The excess caning is trimmed. Then, a tight-fitting piece of reed is glued and hammered into the groove. Its tight pressure provides the final fail-safe for a durable seat or back.

Woodbury University Library
1027 Wilshire Boulevard
Los Angeles, California 90017

Caning being pressed into the router line.

Finishing

Beyond aesthetics, there are several reasons why wood needs to be finished. A proper finish will stabilize moisture content and prevent the wood from shrinking or swelling in response to changes in humidity. Since wood in nature can vary vastly in color, even in different parts of the same tree, finishing is used to create a uniform coloration. And finally, a proper finish will protect wood from dirt and dust, from food or liquid stains.

Wood in its raw state has a dull surface, without luminosity or fully revealed character. Only the expert application of a fine finish can bring out the elegance of a fine wood product.

The end result depends on surface preparation. The finishing process begins with the natural chair frame, once again, being fine sanded. This ensures the removal of any irregularities in the surface that could ruin the clarity and the smooth "hand" of the finished product.

Fillers are used to close the pores of the wood, either a paste or liquid depending on the wood specie. Fillers contain a neutral substance that adheres to the wood without crumbling or changing the coloration. It creates a uniform surface that evenly accepts a stain.

Wood can be given a variety of sheens, from gloss to matte, in a variety of shades.

Walnut oil stain on ash frame.

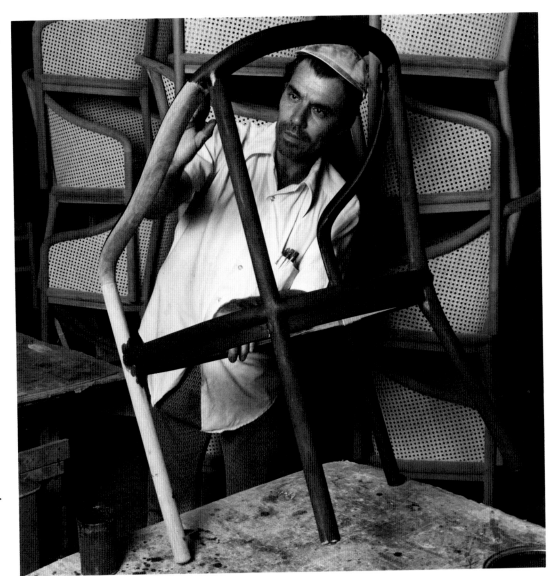

The lacquered chair frame is rubbed down with steel wool. This will be repeated several times in between the thin layers of lacquer.

The application of stain creates long-lasting color since it penetrates deep into the wood cells. Stains come in a variety of media: oil, water, alcohol. They are applied by hand in one or more coats depending on the desired color. After the stain has dried, sealer is applied. When dry, this is sanded — sometimes heavily; as much as half the sealer coat may be sanded off.

Next begins the lacquer application, sprayed on in thin layers and rubbed to the desired sheen with fine steel wool, sand paper, pumice stone, or compound. From one to three layers of lacquer are applied, depending on the finish. Each layer is rubbed with the appropriate substance to render the surface of the lacquer perfectly smooth and clear.

Thus, the final chair frame takes shape, from concept to prototype to finished product. It is now ready for the years of use, which will add to its beauty with the patina of handled and polished wood.

Lacquer applied in spray booth.

Upholstering

Throughout the 18th century the seats and backs of chairs were often upholstered for extra comfort. It was not, however, until the early Victorian period—with the improvement in metal coiled springs and the production of fabrics by the new power looms—that upholstered furniture gained enough importance to give upholsterers a dominant position as style-setters in the furniture business.

In a quality shop of today, the tailoring of upholstery must adhere to strict standards. The most careful attention to detail, even down to a special needle and thread for a particular hand-stitching task, are necessary to ensure a perfectly fitting fabric cover.

The goal is always to provide the correct amount of tension so that the material will neither sag nor pull; to create straight seams and tight pleats with no excess give; to create uniform thicknesses in padding and welting; and above all, to eliminate all open seams, wrinkles, and puckers.

There are many variables in the upholstering process, depending on the style of the chair. However, some general procedures can be pinpointed.

The round carved wood frame armchair shown here requires a fabric application to both the inside and outside of the back. The inside fabric must be applied with precision in order to gracefully cover the cushioning material between it and

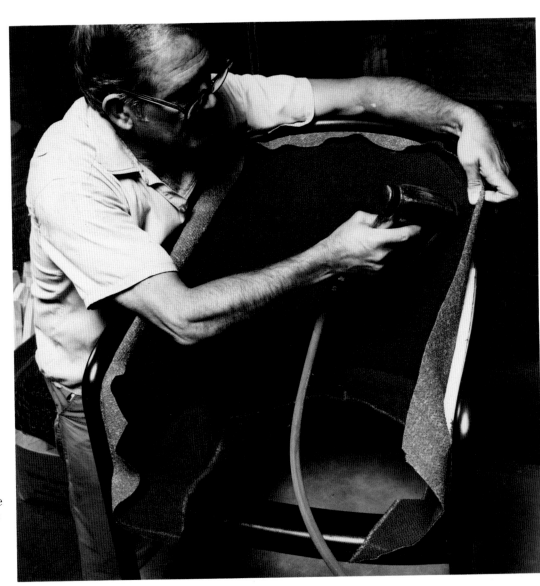

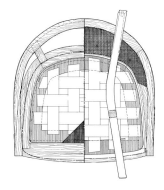

The chair illustrated here is made with a separate seat frame, which is first covered with flexible rubber webbing, polyfoam, and other cushioning materials before the covering material—a fine fabric or leather—is applied.

the outside piece. Some areas of the pre-cut material are dampened so that they will tighten slightly when dried. It must be stretched to the exact tension to procure the proper resilience, and it must be securely fastened inside the wood frame. At this point, the inside shape of the chair will be tested with a template to ensure consistency. The fabric will then be stapled and trimmed. Finally, a length of welting will be applied to the groove between the exposed wood frame and the upholstered parts.

Special standards, as adhered to by Brickel Associates, include use of large fabric pieces where seams are not a desired part of the design, concealed zippers, and painstaking hand molding of the fabric around curves and edges. This, along with other special details, is essential not only to the smooth line of the chair, but for an equal distribution of stress. By dispersing tension equally throughout the fabric, the upholsterer makes his contribution to the longevity of the chair.

**Bankers Chair —
Ward Bennett
1967**

Heavy chairs and furniture have long been used to denote power in executive suites. Cherry wood, with its dark rich patina, is especially reminiscent of traditional settings. The Bankers chair evokes these associations.

In 1967, a major corporation approached Ward Bennett with a special request — to create a chair evocative of the wood-paneled rooms of men's clubs — substantial and traditional, yet light enough in scale to fit into the more contemporary environments of the day. The Bankers chair is that modern interpretation. Fluid in line, the cyma-curve of its crest rail flows into the arms and front legs. This is the most classical of Ward Bennett's designs, used extensively in today's post modernist interiors.

Materials: The French-upholstered chair shown has a natural oiled-cherry frame. It is also made of ash, in a variety of light to dark finishes.

Makers: Brickel Associates Inc., New York.

**Scissor Chair —
Ward Bennett
1968**

The earliest known example of the cruciform frame is thought to be a folding wood stool that originated in Thebes around 1250 B.C. The form was a favorite for 19th century American patent chairs and deck chairs, and in our century provided the theme for Mies van der Rohe's Barcelona chair.

The x-shaped form of the Scissor Chair has appeared in both chairs and stools from ancient Greece and the Renaissance, to Napoleonic France and modern America. While most scissor chairs were originally crafted for convenience and portability, this version was designed entirely for comfort. Self-described by its designer, Ward Bennett, as his most comfortable chair, each critical aspect of the seated human body was considered in its design: the lower back, the angle of the lower leg to the upper leg, etc. While the pitch has been carefully conceived, both its short seat and straight back contribute to its quality of "fitting" all body sizes and types.

Materials: 1¼″ thick round carved ash, finished in a variety of shades from light to dark.

Maker: Brickel Associates Inc., New York.

**Turtle Back—
Ward Bennett
1977**

*In plan view the line of the
arms and back create a shape
from which the name of the
Turtle Back chair derives.
This bow or yoke shape is also
typical of many Chinese
chairs.*

The exposed open frame of
the Turtle Back chair most
clearly reveals one of Bennett's greatest sources of
inspiration—Chinese furniture, in particular, Chinese
chairs. This design is distinguished by the horizontal
line of its lower back which is
parallel to the floor and flows
continuously through the
arms into the front legs. The
crest rail flows directly into
the back legs, so that the
chair form is comprised of
two major interlocking
pieces. There is an obvious
interplay between solid and
void, especially notable in
the open lower part of the
back. The chair requires no
stretchers because its seat
rail is reinforced with a
flange. Therefore while light
in scale, even delicate in
appearance, it is extremely
strong and durable.

Materials: The frame of the
chair shown is 1¼″ thick,
round carved ash, finished in
natural oil, or a variety of
finishes from white ash to
dark oiled walnut.

Maker: Brickel Associates
Inc., New York

University Chair —
Ward Bennett
1978

Conjuring up images of courtrooms and halls of learning, the University chair is a statement of solidity and strength. Considered by Ward Bennett to be his most crafted design — and most difficult to produce — it is also referred to as the "architects" chair, nicknamed so because it has become a favorite of designers and architects.

The all-wood University chair, so named because it was originally designed for the LBJ library at the University of Texas, shows off the craft and materials involved in its making. It is carved from large blocks of solid wood, sculpted to fit the human form, and meticulously joined and finished to reveal the wood's distinctive grain and special quality. Its carved back has an essentially integral crest rail which flows in a continuous line into the arms and front legs. While made entirely of a "hard" material it is one of the most comfortable of Ward Bennett's designs.

Materials: The University chair is carved of ash, and is finished in a variety of light to dark shades.

Maker: Brickel Associates Inc., New York.

Selected Bibliography

Bishop, Robert. *Centuries And Styles Of The American Chair 1640 —1970.* New York: E.P. Dutton & Co., Inc., 1972.

Bjerkoe, Ethel Hall. *The Cabinetmakers of America.* Garden City, New York: Doubleday & Company, Inc., 1957.

Boger, Louise Ade. *Furniture Past & Present.* New York: Doubleday & Company, Inc., 1966.

Bohdan, Carole Lorraine and Volpe, Todd Mitchell. "The Furniture of Gustav Stickley." *Antiques,* May 1977.

Butler, Joseph T. *American Antiques 1800 —1900: A Collector's History and Guide.* New York: Odyssey Press, 1965.

Cathers, David M. *Furniture of the American Arts and Crafts Movement.* New York: New American Library, 1981.

Chippendale, Thomas. *The Gentleman & Cabinet-Maker's Director.* 3rd ed. reprint. New York: Dover Publications, Inc., 1966.

Clark, Robert Judson, ed. *The Arts and Crafts Movement in America 1876 —1916.* Princeton, N.J.: Princeton University Press, 1972.

Comstock, Helen. *American Furniture.* Exton, Pennsylvania: Schiffer Publishing Limited., Copyright by The Viking Press, Inc., 1962.

Davies, Jane B. "Gothic Revival Furniture Designs of Alexander Jackson Davis." *Antiques,* May 1977.

Downs, Joseph. *American Furniture: Queen Anne and Chippendale Periods.* New York: The Macmillan Company, 1952.

Drexler, Arthur. *Charles Eames Furniture from the Design Collection.* New York: The Museum of Modern Art, 1972.

Eastlake, Charles L. *Hints on Household Taste in Furniture, Upholstery, and Other Details.* Boston: James R. Osgood & Company, Late Ticknor & Fields, and Fields, Osgood, & Co., 1877.

Fairbanks, Jonathan L., and Bates, Elizabeth Bidwell. *American Furniture 1620 to the Present.* New York: Richard Marek Publishers, 1981.

Hanks, David A. *The Decorative Designs of Frank Lloyd Wright.* New York: E.P. Dutton, 1979.

_____. *Innovative Furniture in America from 1800 to the Present.* New York: Horizon Press, 1981.

Hepplewhite, George. *The Cabinet-Maker & Upholsterer's Guide.* 3rd ed. reprint. New York: Dover Publications, Inc., 1969.

Kalec, Donald. "The Prairie School Furniture." *Prairie School Review,* 1, Fourth Quarter, 1964.

Kane, Patricia E. *300 Years of American Seating Furniture: Chairs and Beds from the Mabel Brady Garvan and Other Collections at Yale University.* Boston: New York Graphic Society/Little, Brown and Company, 1976.

Kovel, Ralph and Terry. *American Country Furniture 1780 — 1875.* New York: Crown Publishers Inc., 1965.

Lockwood, Luke Vincent. *Colonial Furniture in America.* 2 vols. New York: Charles Scribner's Sons. Rev. ed., 1951.

Makinson, Randell L. *Greene & Greene: Furniture and Related Designs.* Layton, Utah: Peregrine Smith, Inc., 1979.

Meader, Robert F.W. *Illustrated Guide To Shaker Furniture*. New York: Dover Publications, Inc., 1972.

Miller, Edgar G., Jr. *A Book For Amateurs*. Baltimore, Maryland: The Lord Baltimore Press, 1937.

Montgomery, Charles F. *American Furniture: The Federal Period in the Henry Francis du Pont Winterthur Museum*. New York: Viking Press, 1966.

Nakashima, George. *The Soul Of A Tree*. Tokyo, New York, and San Francisco. Kodansha International Ltd., 1981. Distributed in the U.S. through Harper & Row, Publishers.

19th-Century American Furniture and Other Decorative Arts. New York: The Metropolitan Museum of Art, 1970.

Nineteenth Century Furniture: Innovation, Revival. Introduction by Mary Jean Madigan. New York: An Art & Antiques Book, 1982.

Nutting, Wallace. *Furniture of the Pilgrim Century*. Two Vols., reprint. New York: Dover Publications, Inc. 1965.

O'Gorman, James F. *H.H. Richardson and His Office: A Centennial of His Move to Boston 1874*. Cambridge, Mass.: Department of Printing and Graphic Arts, Harvard College Library, 1974.

Ormsbee, Thomas H. *Field Guide to American Victorian Furniture*. Boston: Little, Brown and Company, 1952.

_____. Field Guide to Early American Furniture. Boston: Little, Brown and Company, 1951.

Page, Marian. *Furniture Designed By Architects*. New York: Whitney Library of Design, an imprint of Watson—Guptill Publications, and London: The Architectural Press Ltd. 1980.

Russell, Frank. *A Century of Chair Design*. New York: Rizzoli, 1980.

Santore, Charles. *The Windsor Style in America 1730—1830*. Philadelphia, Pennsylvania: Running Press, 1981.

Sheraton, Thomas. *The Cabinet-Maker and Upholsterer's Drawing-Book*. 3rd rev. ed. Reprint. Charles F. Montgomery and Wilfred P. Cole, eds. New York: Praeger Publishers, 1970.

Stickley, Gustav. *Stickley, Craftsman Furniture Catalogs*. New York: Dover Publications, Inc. 1979.

Schwartz, Marvin D. *American Furniture of the Colonial Period*. New York: Metropolitan Museum of Art, 1976.

Schwartz, Marvin D.; Stanek, Edward J.; and True, Douglas K. *The Furniture of John Henry Belter and The Rococo Revival*. New York: E.P. Dutton. 1981.

Credits

Style Survey and Glossary—unless otherwise noted below, all line illustrations done by Jim Silks and Randall Lieu. Photographs and drawings have been reproduced courtesy of the following publications, individuals and institutions:

Cover
Wood butts. Photograph by Amos T.S. Chan.

Page 5
Top right: The Turner. An illustration from *The Book of Trades or Library of Useful Arts. 1807.*

Page 12
Top right: Connecticut Chippendale splat back variations. From Thomas Chippendale's *The Gentleman and Cabinet Maker's Director.* Courtesy of The Furniture World/Furniture South and The Furniture Library.

Page 17
Top right: Hepplewhite shield back variations. From George Hepplewhite's *The Cabinet-Maker and Upholsterer's Guide.* Courtesy of The Furniture World/Furniture South and The Furniture Library.

Page 18
Top right: Sheraton square back variations. From Thomas Sheraton's *The Cabinet-Maker and Upholsterer's Drawing Book.* Courtesy of The Furniture World/Furniture South and The Furniture Library.

Page 19
Top right: Duncan Phyfe sketch. Courtesy of Henry Francis du Pont Winterthur Museum, Joseph Downs Manuscript Collection, No. 56 x 6.4.

Page 20
Top right: Paper label of Charles Honoré Lannuier. Courtesy of The Metropolitan Museum of Art, Rogers Fund, 1953 (53.181). All rights reserved, The Metropolitan Museum Of Art.

Page 21
Top right: Hitchcock stencil-back variations. Courtesy of the Hitchcock Chair Company, Riverton, Ct. Photograph from The Picture Collection, Cooper-Hewitt Museum Library: Smithsonian Institution, New York.

Page 27
Top right: Davis's study for Wheelback Chair. Courtesy of Museum of The City of New York.

Page 32
Top right: Louis XVI Revival leg variation. From Thomas Sheraton's *The Cabinet Maker and Upholsterer's Drawing Book.* Courtesy of The Furniture World/Furniture South and The Furniture Library.

Page 34
Top right: Turkish upholstered parlor furniture. From the 1897 Spring Catalog—Sears, Roebuck and Company. Courtesy of Sears, Roebuck and Company, Chicago, Illinois.

Page 35
Top right: Richardson's drawing. Courtesy of The Houghton Library, Harvard University, Cambridge, Massachusetts.

Page 36
Top right: Shaker slat back chairs. Photograph courtesy of Robert F.W. Meader.

Page 37
Top right: Log cedar settee, Rustic Construction Works. Courtesy of The Picture Collection, Cooper-Hewitt Museum Library: Smithsonian Institution, New York.

Page 40
Top right: Mortise-and-tenon construction detail. From *Craftsman Magazine*. Photograph courtesy of Peter Curran.

Page 41
Top right: Ellis rendering. From *Craftsman Magazine*. Photograph courtesy of Peter Curran.

Page 42
Top right: Robie House dining chair elevation drawing. Illustration by David T. Van Zanten. Courtesy of the Historic American Building Survey, Library of Congress; and The University of Chicago—Frank Lloyd Wright Robie House, Chicago, Illinois.

Page 43
Top right: Chair back variations with peg work. Photograph for illustration courtesy of The Picture Collection, Cooper-Hewitt Museum Library: Smithsonian Institution, New York.

Page 44
Top right: Elmslie drawing. Courtesy of Northwest Architectural Archives, University of Minnesota, Minneapolis.

Page 45
Top right: Photograph, Saarinen dining room chair. Photography by Steven Rost courtesy of Cranbrook Academy of Art/Museum, Bloomfield Hills, Michigan.

Page 46
Top right: Molded plywood parts before assembly. Photograph by Charles Eames. Courtesy of The Office Of Charles and Ray Eames, Venice, California.

Page 47
Top right: Library steps. Courtesy of Mrs. Curtis Bok, Philadelphia, Pa. Photograph for illustration courtesy of the National Museum of American Art, Smithsonian Institution, Washington, D.C.

Page 49
Top right: ¾ back view of Pull-up Chair, Brickel Associates Inc. Photograph by Michael Pateman.

Making a Wood Chair—unless otherwise noted below, all photographs done by Amos T.S. Chan. All other photographs and illustrations have been reproduced courtesy of the following publications, individuals, and institutions:

Pages 82/83
Ward Bennett in the Scissor Chair. Photograph by Michael Pateman.

Page 84
Top left: Drawing of Pull-up Chair, Brickel Associates Inc. Illustration by Norman Diekman.

Page 86
Top right: Saw cut log illustration. Reprinted by permission from *Masonry, Carpentry, Joinery*. Copyright © 1980 by Chicago Review Press.

Page 92
Top right: Dowelled joint illustration. Reprinted by permission from *Masonry, Carpentry, Joinery*. Copyright © 1980 by Chicago Review Press.

Credits *continued*

Page 100
Top left: Cane pattern. Illustration by Jim Silks and Randall Lieu.

Page 105
Top right: Section drawing of Pull-up Chair, Brickel Associates Inc. Illustration by Norman Diekman.

Page 106
Bankers Chair, Brickel Associates Inc., ¾ front view and detail. Photographs by Michael Pateman.

Page 107
Scissor Chair, Brickel Associates Inc., ¾ front view and detail. Photographs by Michael Pateman.

Page 108
Turtle Back Chair, Brickel Associates Inc., ¾ front view and overhead view. Photographs by Michael Pateman.

Page 109
University Chair, Brickel Associates Inc., ¾ front view. Photograph by Michael Pateman.

Notes

[1] Quoted in *The Cabinetmakers of America*, Ethel Hall Bjerkoe, Doubleday & Co., New York, 1957, p. 172.

[2] William Morris's lecture on "Gothic Architecture" to the Arts and Crafts Society in 1889 reprinted in *Centenary Edition* of William Morris's stories, poems, lectures, and essays, edited by G.D.H. Cole for the Nonesuch Press, London, 1948, Random House, New York, p. 475.

[3] J. Newtown Nind and Gustav Stickley, "Modern Mission and Craftsman Furniture" in *The Furniture Styles*, edited by Herbert Binstead, Trade Periodical Co. 1901, p. 186.

[4] Ibid, p. 179.

[5] *The Craftsman* magazine, December 1909.

[6] Quoted in *Furniture Designed by Architects*, Marian Page, Whitney Library of Design, New York, 1980, p. 123.

[7] *Wooden Works, furniture objects by five contemporary craftsmen*, exhibition catalog organized by The Renwick Gallery, published by Minnesota Museum of Art, St. Paul 1972, p. 24.

[8] Ibid. p. 24.

[9] Ibid, p. 22.

[10] Ibid, p. 4.

[11] Ibid, p. 6.

[12] *Masonry, Carpentry, Joinery*, Chicago Review Press, Chicago, 1980, p. 11.